Microsoft

MOS 2013 Study Guide
for Microsoft Outlook

Joan Lambert

D1537871

PUBLISHED BY
Microsoft Press
A Division of Microsoft Corporation
One Microsoft Way
Redmond, Washington 98052-6399

Library of Congress Control Number: 2013941815
ISBN: 978-0-7356-6922-2

Printed and bound in the United States of America.

Third Printing: September 2014

Microsoft Press books are available through booksellers and distributors worldwide. If you need support related to this book, email Microsoft Press Book Support at mspinput@microsoft.com. Please tell us what you think of this book at http://www.microsoft.com/learning/booksurvey.

Microsoft and the trademarks listed at http://www.microsoft.com/en-us/legal/intellectualproperty/trademarks/en-us.aspx are trademarks of the Microsoft group of companies. All other marks are property of their respective owners.

The example companies, organizations, products, domain names, email addresses, logos, people, places, and events depicted herein are fictitious. No association with any real company, organization, product, domain name, email address, logo, person, place, or event is intended or should be inferred.

Acquisitions Editor: Rosemary Caperton
Editorial Production: Online Training Solutions, Inc. (OTSI)
Technical Reviewer: Rob Carr (OTSI)
Copyeditors: Kathy Krause and Jaime Odell (OTSI)
Indexer: Krista Wall (OTSI)
Cover: Microsoft Press Brand Team

Contents

What do you think of this book? We want to hear from you!

Microsoft is interested in hearing your feedback so we can continually improve our books and learning resources for you. To participate in a brief online survey, please visit:

microsoft.com/learning/booksurvey

3   Manage schedules   85

What do you think of this book? We want to hear from you!

Microsoft is interested in hearing your feedback so we can continually improve our books and learning resources for you. To participate in a brief online survey, please visit:

microsoft.com/learning/booksurvey

Introduction

The Microsoft Office Specialist (MOS) certification program has been designed to validate your knowledge of and ability to use programs in the Microsoft Office 2013 suite of programs, Microsoft Office 365, and Microsoft SharePoint. This book has been designed to guide you in studying the types of tasks you are likely to be required to demonstrate in Exam 77-423: Microsoft Outlook 2013.

Who this book is for

MOS 2013 Study Guide for Microsoft Outlook is designed for experienced computer users seeking Microsoft Office Specialist certification in Outlook 2013.

The MOS exams for individual programs are practical rather than theoretical. You must demonstrate that you can complete certain tasks or projects rather than simply answering questions about program features. The successful MOS certification candidate will have at least six months of experience using all aspects of the application on a regular basis—for example, using Outlook at work or school to create and send messages, format message content, organize and manage messages, schedule appointments and events, manage meetings, create notes and journal entries, track tasks, store contact information, locate information, and print and save information. You should also know how to customize Outlook settings and automate tasks within Outlook.

As a certification candidate, you probably have a lot of experience with the program you want to become certified in. Many of the procedures described in this book will be familiar to you; others might not be. Read through each study section and ensure that you are familiar with not only the procedures included in the section, but also the concepts and tools discussed in the review information. In some cases, graphics depict the tools you will use to perform procedures related to the skill set. Study the graphics and ensure that you are familiar with all the options available for each tool.

How this book is organized

The exam coverage is divided into chapters representing broad skill sets that correlate to the functional groups covered by the exam, and each chapter is divided into sections addressing groups of related skills that correlate to the exam objectives. Each section includes review information, generic procedures, and practice tasks you can complete on your own while studying. When necessary, we provide practice files you can use to work through the practice tasks. You can practice the procedures in this book by using the practice files supplied or by using your own files.

Download the practice files

Before you can complete the practice tasks in this book, you need to download the book's practice files to your computer. These practice files can be downloaded from the following page:

http://aka.ms/mosOutlook2013/files

> **Important** The Outlook 2013 program is not available from this website. You should purchase and install that program before using this book.

If you would like to be able to refer to the completed versions of practice files at a later time, you can save the practice files that you modify while working through the practice tasks in this book. If you save your changes and later want to repeat the practice task, you can download the original practice files again.

The following table lists the practice files for this book.

Folder and chapter	Files
MOSOutlook2013\Objective1 1 Manage the Outlook environment	n/a
MOSOutlook2013\Objective2 2 Manage messages	*Outlook_2-1a.docx* *Outlook_2-1b.pptx* *Outlook_2-2.docx*
MOSOutlook2013\Objective3 3 Manage schedules	*Outlook_3-2.docx*
MOSOutlook2013\Objective4 4 Manage contacts and groups	*Outlook_4-1.png*

Adapting exercise steps

The screen images shown in this book were captured at a screen resolution of 1024 × 768, at 100 percent magnification. If your settings are different, the ribbon on your screen might not look the same as the one shown in this book. For example, you might have more or fewer buttons in each of the groups, the buttons you have might be represented by larger or smaller icons than those shown, or the group might be represented by a button that you click to display the group's commands. As a result, exercise instructions that involve the ribbon might require a little adaptation. Our instructions use this format:

- On the **Insert** tab, in the **Illustrations** group, click the **Chart** button.

If the command is in a list or on a menu, our instructions use this format:

- On the **Home** tab, in the **Editing** group, click the **Find** arrow, and then click **Advanced Find**.

> **Tip** On subsequent instances of instructions located on the same tab or in the same group, the instructions are simplified to reflect that we've already established the working location.

If differences between your display settings and ours cause a button to appear differently on your screen from the way it does in this book, you can easily adapt the steps to locate the command. First click the specified tab, and then locate the specified group. If a group has been collapsed into a group list or under a group button, click the list or button to display the group's commands. If you can't immediately identify the button you want, point to likely candidates to display their names in ScreenTips.

If you prefer not to have to adapt the steps, set up your screen to match ours while you read and work through the exercises in this book.

In this book, we provide instructions based on the traditional keyboard and mouse input methods. If you're using the program on a touch-enabled device, you might be giving commands by tapping with a stylus or your finger. If so, substitute a tapping action any time we instruct you to click a user interface element. Also note that when we tell you to enter information, you can do so by typing on a keyboard, tapping an on-screen keyboard, or even speaking aloud, depending on your computer setup and your personal preferences.

Ebook edition

If you're reading the ebook edition of this book, you can do the following:

- Search the full text
- Print
- Copy and paste

You can purchase and download the ebook edition from:

http://aka.ms/mosOutlook2013

Get support and give feedback

The following sections provide information about getting help with this book and contacting us to provide feedback or report errors.

Errata

We've made every effort to ensure the accuracy of this book and its companion content. Any errors that have been reported since this book was published are listed at:

http://aka.ms/mosOutlook2013/errata

If you find an error that is not already listed, you can report it to us through the same page.

If you need additional support, email Microsoft Press Book Support from:

mspinput@microsoft.com.

Please note that product support for Microsoft software is not offered through the addresses above.

We want to hear from you

At Microsoft Press, your satisfaction is our top priority, and your feedback our most valuable asset. Please tell us what you think of this book from:

http://www.microsoft.com/learning/booksurvey

The survey is short, and we read every one of your comments and ideas. Thanks in advance for your input!

Stay in touch

Let's keep the conversation going! We're on Twitter at:

http://twitter.com/MicrosoftPress

Taking a Microsoft Office Specialist exam

Desktop computing proficiency is increasingly important in today's business world. When screening, hiring, and training employees, employers can feel reassured by relying on the objectivity and consistency of technology certification to ensure the competence of their workforce. As an employee or job seeker, you can use technology certification to prove that you already have the skills you need to succeed, saving current and future employers the time and expense of training you.

Microsoft Office Specialist certification

Microsoft Office Specialist certification is designed to assist employees in validating their skills with Office programs. The following certification paths are available:

- A Microsoft Office Specialist (MOS) is an individual who has demonstrated proficiency by passing a certification exam in one or more Office programs, including Microsoft Word, Excel, PowerPoint, Outlook, Access, OneNote, or SharePoint.

- A Microsoft Office Specialist Expert (MOS Expert) is an individual who has demonstrated that he or she has mastered the more advanced features of Word or Excel by passing the required certification exams.

- A Microsoft Office Specialist Master (MOS Master) is an individual who has demonstrated that he or she has mastered multiple Office applications by passing the MOS Expert certification exams for Word and Excel, the MOS certification exam for PowerPoint, and one additional MOS certification exam.

Choosing a certification path

When deciding which certifications you would like to pursue, you should assess the following:

- The program and program versions with which you are familiar
- The length of time you have used the program and how frequently you use it
- Whether you have had formal or informal training in the use of that program
- Whether you use most or all of the available program features
- Whether you are considered a go-to resource by business associates, friends, and family members who have difficulty with the program

Candidates for MOS-level certification are expected to successfully complete a wide range of standard business tasks, such as formatting a document or worksheet and its content; creating and formatting visual content; or working with SharePoint lists, libraries, Web Parts, and dashboards. Successful candidates generally have six or more months of experience with the specific Office program, including either formal, instructor-led training or self-study using MOS-approved books, guides, or interactive computer-based materials.

Candidates for MOS Expert–level certification are expected to successfully complete more complex tasks that involve using the advanced functionality of the program. Successful candidates generally have at least six months, and may have several years, of experience with the programs, including formal, instructor-led training or self-study using MOS-approved materials.

Test-taking tips

Every MOS certification exam is developed from a set of exam skill standards (referred to as the *objective domain*) that are derived from studies of how the Office programs are used in the workplace. Because these skill standards dictate the scope of each exam, they provide critical information about how to prepare for certification. This book follows the structure of the published exam objectives; see "How this book is organized" in the Introduction for more information.

The MOS certification exams are performance based and require you to complete business-related tasks or projects in the program for which you are seeking certification. For example, you might be presented with a file and told to do something specific with it, or presented with a sample document and told to create it by using resources provided for that purpose. Your score on the exam reflects how well you perform the requested tasks or complete the project within the allotted time.

Here is some helpful information about taking the exam:

- Keep track of the time. Your exam time does not officially begin until after you finish reading the instructions provided at the beginning of the exam. During the exam, the amount of time remaining is shown at the bottom of the exam interface. You can't pause the exam after you start it.

- Pace yourself. At the beginning of the exam, you will receive information about the questions or projects that are included in the exam. Some questions will require that you complete more than one task. Each project will require that you complete multiple tasks. During the exam, the amount of time remaining to complete the questions or project, and the number of completed and remaining questions if applicable, is shown at the bottom of the exam interface.

- Read the exam instructions carefully before beginning. Follow all the instructions provided completely and accurately.

- Enter requested information as it appears in the instructions, but without duplicating the formatting unless you are specifically instructed to do so. For example, the text and values you are asked to enter might appear in the instructions in bold and underlined text, but you should enter the information without applying these formats.

- Close all dialog boxes before proceeding to the next exam question unless you are specifically instructed not to do so.

- Don't close task panes before proceeding to the next exam question unless you are specifically instructed to do so.

- If you are asked to print a document, worksheet, chart, report, or slide, perform the task, but be aware that nothing will actually be printed.

- When performing tasks to complete a project-based exam, save your work frequently.

- Don't worry about extra keystrokes or mouse clicks. Your work is scored based on its result, not on the method you use to achieve that result (unless a specific method is indicated in the instructions).

- If a computer problem occurs during the exam (for example, if the exam does not respond or the mouse no longer functions) or if a power outage occurs, contact a testing center administrator immediately. The administrator will restart the computer and return the exam to the point where the interruption occurred, with your score intact.

Certification benefits

At the conclusion of the exam, you will receive a score report, indicating whether you passed the exam. If your score meets or exceeds the passing standard (the minimum required score), you will be contacted by email by the Microsoft Certification Program team. The email message you receive will include your Microsoft Certification ID and links to online resources, including the Microsoft Certified Professional site. On this site, you can download or order a printed certificate, create a virtual business card, order an ID card, view and share your certification transcript, access the Logo Builder, and access other useful and interesting resources, including special offers from Microsoft and affiliated companies.

Depending on the level of certification you achieve, you will qualify to display one of three logos on your business card and other personal promotional materials. These logos attest to the fact that you are proficient in the applications or cross-application skills necessary to achieve the certification.

Microsoft
Office Specialist
Microsoft
Office Specialist Expert
Microsoft
Office Specialist Master

Using the Logo Builder, you can create a personalized certification logo that includes the MOS logo and the specific programs in which you have achieved certification. If you achieve MOS certification in multiple programs, you can include multiple certifications in one logo.

For more information

To learn more about the Microsoft Office Specialist exams and related courseware, visit:

http://www.microsoft.com/learning/en/us/mos-certification.aspx

Microsoft
Outlook 2013

This part of the book covers the skills you need to have for certification as a Microsoft Office Specialist in Microsoft Outlook 2013. Specifically, you need to be able to complete tasks that demonstrate the following skill sets:

1 Manage the Outlook environment

2 Manage messages

3 Manage schedules

4 Manage contacts and groups

With these skills, you can efficiently manage communications with colleagues and perform the scheduling and tracking tasks that are important to working efficiently in a business environment.

Prerequisites

We assume that you have been working with Outlook 2013 for at least six months and that you know how to perform fundamental tasks that are not specifically mentioned in the objectives for this Microsoft Office Specialist exam. Before you begin studying for this exam, you might want to make sure you are familiar with the information in this section.

Work in individual modules

Mail module

Each time you start Outlook and connect to your email server, any new messages received since the last time you connected appear in your Inbox. Depending on your settings, Outlook downloads either the entire message to your computer or only the message header. The headers, which are listed in the content pane to the right of the Folder Pane, provide basic information about the message, such as:

- The item type (such as message, meeting request, or task assignment).
- The sender, recipient, and subject.
- The most recent response type.
- If it has attachments.
- If it has been digitally signed or encrypted.
- If it has been marked as being of high or low importance.

Messages you haven't yet read are indicated by vertical blue lines and bold headers. You can view the text of a message in several ways:

→ You can open a message in its own window by double-clicking its header in the message list.

→ You can read a message without opening it by clicking its header in the message list to display the message in the Reading Pane.

Calendar module

When you display the Calendar module, the Folder Pane changes to display the Date Navigator and a list of the local, Microsoft Exchange Server, Microsoft SharePoint, and Internet calendars that Outlook is configured to connect to.

People module

In the People module, the Folder Pane displays a list of the available address books. On the contact index to the right of the content pane in the People module, you can click alphabetic buttons to quickly jump to contact records filed by a specific letter.

Tasks, Notes, and Journal modules

In the Tasks module, the Folder Pane displays the available task folders and task folder views. In the Notes module, it displays the available note folders. In the Journal module, it displays the Folder List.

> **Tip** You can display the Mail, Calendar, People, Tasks, and Notes modules from the Navigation Bar at the bottom of the Folder Pane. You can display the Journal module by pressing Ctrl+8, or by displaying the Folder List in the Folder Pane and then clicking the Journal folder.

Switch views

You can use commands on the View tab of the ribbon to display different views of module content. If none of the standard views meets your needs, you can click the View Settings button in the Current View group on the View tab to define a custom view of the information in the current module.

Create Outlook items

You can create any type of Outlook item from any module. You can also create folders to contain items such as mail messages, calendar information, or contact records. You must specify the type of items the folder will contain when you create it.

> ➤ **To create an item specific to the current module**
>
> → On the **Home** tab, in the **New** group, click the **New *Item*** button.
>
> → Press **Ctrl+N**.

> **Tip** The New button always creates the default item for the current module. For example, in the Mail module, the New button and keyboard shortcut create a new message.

> ➤ **To create any item from any module**
>
> → On the **Home** tab, in the **New** group, click the **New Items** button, and then click the type of item you want to create.
>
> → Press **Ctrl+Shift+M** to create a message.
>
> → Press **Ctrl+Shift+A** to create an appointment.
>
> → Press **Ctrl+Shift+Q** to create a meeting.
>
> → Press **Ctrl+Shift+C** to create a contact.
>
> → Press **Ctrl+Shift+L** to create a contact group.
>
> → Press **Ctrl+Shift+K** to create a task.
>
> → Press **Ctrl+Shift+N** to create a note.

➤ **To create a folder**

1. On the **Folder** tab, in the **New** group, click the **New Folder** button; or press **Ctrl+E**.

2. In the **Create New Folder** dialog box, enter a name for the folder in the **Name** box, and then in the **Folder contains** list, click **Calendar Items**, **Contact Items**, **InfoPath Form Items**, **Journal Items**, **Mail and Post Items**, **Note Items**, or **Task Items**.

3. In the **Select where to place the folder** list, click the location in which you want to create the folder.

4. In the **Create New Folder** dialog box, click **OK**.

Address messages

To address an email message, enter the intended recipient's email address into the To box. If you want to send a message to more than one person, separate the addresses with semicolons. If a message recipient's address is in your address book, you can enter the person's name, and Outlook will look for the corresponding email address. (You can either wait for Outlook to validate the name or press Ctrl+K to immediately validate the names and addresses you enter.)

As you enter characters in the To, Cc, or Bcc box, Outlook might display matching addresses in a list below the box. Select a name or email address from the list and then press Tab or Enter to insert the entire name or address in the box.

If your email account is part of an Exchange Server network, you can send messages to another person on the same network by entering only his or her email alias (for example, joan)—the at symbol (@) and domain name aren't required.

By default, Outlook searches your Global Address List and main address book, but you can instruct the program to search other address books as well. If no address book contains an entry for the name you entered, when you send the message, Outlook prompts you to select an address book entry or create a new contact.

➤ **To have Outlook search additional address books**

1. On the **Home** tab, in the **Find** group, click **Address Book**.

2. In the **Address Book** window, on the **Tools** menu, click **Options**.

3. In the **Addressing** dialog box, click **Custom**, and then click **Add**.

4. In the **Add Address List** dialog box, click the address list you want to add, click **Add**, and then click **Close**.

5. In the **Addressing** dialog box, click **OK**, and then close the **Address Book** window.

1 Manage the Outlook environment

The skills tested in this section of the Microsoft Office Specialist exam for Microsoft Outlook 2013 relate to managing the Outlook environment. Specifically, the following objectives are associated with this set of skills:

1.1 Customize Outlook settings

1.2 Automate Outlook

1.3 Print and save information in Outlook

1.4 Search in Outlook

The goal of the Office 2013 working environment is to make working with content, including that of Microsoft Word documents, Excel workbooks, PowerPoint presentations, Outlook email messages, and Access database tables, as intuitive as possible. To that end, each program in the Office system, including Outlook, has a similar user interface.

Unlike other Office programs, Outlook doesn't function for a single purpose or create a single category of files. You use it to create, organize, and track several types of information that are critical to keeping your daily life functioning smoothly. To minimize the work of dealing with such diverse items of information as email messages, contact records, appointments, tasks, and notes, Outlook provides a module for each type and presents each module in a similar interface, making it possible for you to work with different items of information in consistent ways.

This chapter guides you in studying ways of customizing Outlook, configuring settings, and automating processes to fit the way you work. In addition, this chapter guides you in studying ways of performing operations such as printing, saving, and searching that are common across all Outlook modules.

> **Practice Files** You don't need any practice files to complete the practice tasks in this chapter.

1.1 Customize Outlook settings

Customize the appearance of the program window

You can control the display, and in some cases the location, of program window elements from the View tab of each module. In addition to the title bar, ribbon, and status bar that are common to all Office programs, the Outlook program window includes four areas in which you work with Outlook items.

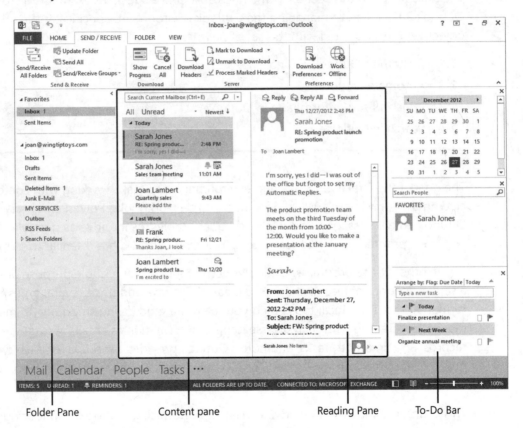

Folder Pane   Content pane   Reading Pane   To-Do Bar

The four content areas of the Outlook program window are as follows:

- **Folder Pane** This collapsible pane appears on the left side of the Outlook program window in every module. Its contents change depending on the module you're viewing—it might display links to email folders, Microsoft SharePoint lists and libraries, external content, or view options. By default, the Folder Pane is minimized to display only favorite folders. The Folder Pane state (minimized or expanded) remains the same as you switch among modules.

   When the compact Navigation Bar is displayed, it is incorporated into the Folder Pane and displayed vertically when the Folder Pane is minimized or horizontally when the Folder Pane is open.

- **Content pane** The content pane is the part of the program window bordered on the left by the Folder Pane and on the right by the To-Do Bar when the To-Do Bar is displayed, or by the right side of the program window when it is not displayed. The content pane displays the content of the selected module—your message list, calendar, contact records, or tasks—and can also host the Reading Pane.

- **Reading Pane** This optional pane can be displayed vertically or horizontally within the content pane. Within the Reading Pane, you can preview and work with the content of a selected item, or display a full-featured preview of a file that is attached to an Outlook item (including Microsoft Word documents, Excel worksheets, PowerPoint presentations, and PDF files). The Reading Pane can also host the People Pane.

   The Reading Pane can be displayed in any Outlook module but is displayed by default only in the Mail and Tasks modules.

- **To-Do Bar** This optional pane can display a monthly calendar, favorite contacts, and your task list, or any combination of these that you choose. In Outlook 2013, the To-Do Bar can be either open or closed, but not minimized as it could be in previous versions of Outlook.

   The To-Do Bar can be displayed in any Outlook module, but is not displayed by default in any module.

The Navigation Bar, which is new in Outlook 2013, is located near the lower-left corner of the program window, above the status bar. In previous versions of Outlook, the navigation controls were incorporated into the Folder Pane (formerly called the Navigation Pane). In Outlook 2013, the navigation controls are presented on the Navigation Bar, which can appear as a compact vertical or horizontal bar that displays only module icons, or as a larger horizontal bar with text labels.

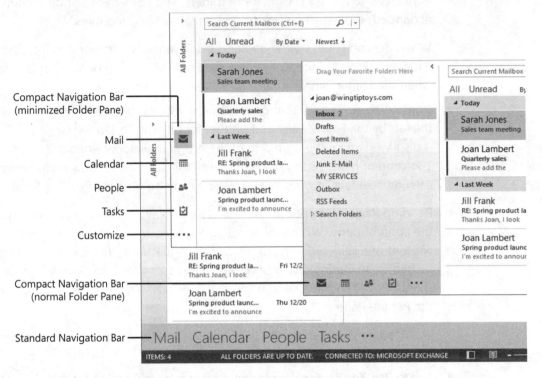

You can display the Mail, Calendar, People, and Tasks modules by clicking the corresponding button on the Navigation Bar. If a module name doesn't appear on the Navigation Bar, click the ellipsis at the right end of the Navigation Bar, and then click the module name to display it.

> **Tip** You can access the Journal from the Folder List in the Folder Pane, or by pressing Ctrl+8.

You can "peek" at the current content of the Calendar, People, or Tasks module by pointing to the module button. *Peeks* display information that in previous versions of Outlook was shown only on the To-Do Bar. The Calendar peek displays this month's Date Navigator and today's appointments, the People peek displays the contacts you've saved as favorites and a search box, and the Tasks peek displays your upcoming tasks and a task entry box. Clicking the Dock The Peek button in the upper-right corner of any peek pane pins the peek to the To-Do Bar (and displays the To-Do Bar in the program window, if it wasn't already open).

Dock the peek

You can change the appearance of the Navigation Bar and the modules that are displayed on it from the Navigation Options dialog box.

The compact Navigation Bar is incorporated into the Folder Pane and its orientation depends on whether the Folder Pane is minimized or expanded. The standard Navigation Bar is separate from the Folder Pane and does not change orientation. To display more or fewer buttons on the standard Navigation Bar, modify the settings in the Navigation Options dialog box.

➤ **To display or close the Folder Pane**

➜ On the **View** tab, in the **Layout** group, click the **Folder Pane** button, and then click **Normal** to display the pane or **Off** to hide it.

➤ **To minimize or expand the Folder Pane**

➜ On the **View** tab, in the **Layout** group, click the **Folder Pane** button, and then click **Minimized**.

➜ At the top of the **Folder Pane**, click the **Minimize the Folder Pane** button or the **Expand the Folder Pane** button.

➜ Click the **All Folders** button on the minimized **Folder Pane** to temporarily expand it.

➤ **To change the width of the Folder Pane or To-Do Bar**

➜ Drag the divider between the **Folder Pane** or **To-Do Bar** and the content pane to the right or left.

➤ **To switch between the compact and standard Navigation Bar**

1. On the **Navigation Bar**, click the ellipsis, and then click **Navigation Options**.

2. In the **Navigation Options** dialog box, select or clear the **Compact Navigation** check box, and then click **OK**.

➤ **To change the number of buttons on the Navigation Bar**

➜ To display more or fewer buttons on the vertical compact **Navigation Bar**, drag its top border up or down up.

➜ To display more or fewer buttons on the horizontal compact **Navigation Bar**, change the width of the **Folder Pane**.

Or

1. On the **Navigation Bar**, click the ellipsis, and then click **Navigation Options**.

2. In the **Navigation Options** dialog box, set the maximum number of visible items (you can display up to eight), and then click **OK**.

> ➤ **To change the order of buttons on the Navigation Bar**

  → In the **Navigation Options** dialog box, move module names up and down in the **Display in this order** box to set the order of the module buttons from left to right on the **Navigation Bar**.

Configure program options

You can change many of the default program settings from the Outlook Options dialog box. From this dialog box, you can control the settings and appearance of many Outlook features, including the following:

- Email accounts, functionality, and formatting

- Editorial and archive functions

- The Folder Pane and Reading Pane

- Your calendar, task list, and address books

- The indexing and search functions

- Message flagging

- The content of the Quick Access Toolbar and ribbon

The Outlook Options dialog box is divided into eight pages of function-specific settings, two pages of feature-specific settings (for the ribbon and for the Quick Access Toolbar), and two pages of security-related settings.

> **Important** The Microsoft Office Specialist exam for Outlook 2013 includes objectives related to specific settings that are documented individually in this book. However, the Outlook Options dialog box contains other options not included on the exam, which are not covered in this book. Be sure to look through the Outlook Options dialog box for options you might be interested in using.

➤ **To open the Outlook Options dialog box**

→ In the left pane of the **Backstage** view, click **Options**.

Set defaults for outgoing messages

The fonts, styles, colors, and backgrounds of content you create in Outlook are governed by a theme. The default theme is named *Office*. The default settings use a black font for new messages and a blue font for message responses (replies and forwards).

You can change the appearance of message content by changing the theme of the individual message, by applying styles to paragraphs, or by applying local character and paragraph formatting. In addition to formatting messages on a case by case basis, you can change the default look of all new messages by choosing a different theme. If you're happy with the basic theme but want to change the default appearance of text, you can separately specify the font, size, style, and color of the text of new messages, responses and forwarded messages, and messages sent in Plain Text format. You can continue to use different colors to visually differentiate between original message content and your responses within a message trail. Or you might prefer to keep things clean and simple, and always use the same font regardless of whether a message is new; this simpler approach can help recipients to recognize message content from you.

> **Tip** You set the default appearance of plain text message content in the Signatures And Stationery box. You cannot apply additional font formatting or paragraph formatting to plain text content.

You select message fonts and control other aspects of message responses on the Personal Stationery page of the Signatures And Stationery dialog box.

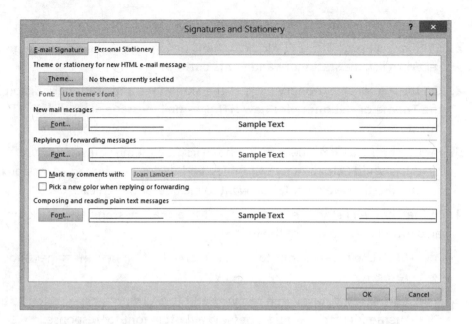

When you respond to a message, Outlook inserts the original message below a blank area. You can enter your response in the blank area, or you can respond inline, within the body of the original message. If you respond inline, you can insert identifying text, such as *[your name]*, before your responses so that the recipient can easily locate them. You can also have Outlook select a color for your response text to differentiate it from text that was in the previous message.

You configure some of these options from the Mail page of the Outlook Options dialog box.

➤ **To specify an email theme or stationery for HTML messages**

1. On the **Mail** page of the **Outlook Options** dialog box, in the **Compose messages** section, click the **Stationery and Fonts** button.

2. On the **Personal Stationery** page of the **Signatures and Stationery** dialog box, in the **Theme or stationery for new HTML e-mail message** area, click the **Theme** button.

3. In the **Theme or Stationery** dialog box, click the theme you want to use. Select or clear the **Vivid Colors**, **Active Graphics**, and **Background Image** check boxes to specify the theme elements you want to include, and then click **OK**.

4. In the **Theme or stationery for new HTML e-mail message** area, click the **Font** arrow, and then do one of the following:

   ○ Click **Use theme's font** to use the theme font for new messages and responses.

   ○ Click **Use my font when replying and forwarding messages** to use the theme font for new messages and a custom font for responses.

   ○ Click **Always use my font** to use a custom font for all messages and to use only the styles, colors, and backgrounds of the selected theme.

5. In the **Signatures and Stationery** dialog box, click **OK**.

➤ **To reset to the default theme**

1. On the **Personal Stationery** page of the **Signatures and Stationery** dialog box, in the **Theme or stationery for new HTML e-mail message** area, click the **Theme** button.

2. In the **Theme or Stationery** dialog box, click **(No Theme)**, and then click **OK**.

➤ **To set the font for specific message types**

1. On the **Personal Stationery** page of the **Signatures and Stationery** dialog box, click the **Font** button corresponding to the type of message for which you want to format the font.

2. In the **Font** dialog box, select the font, style, size, effects, and advanced formatting of the font you want to use, and then click **OK**.

3. In the **Signatures and Stationery** dialog box, click **OK**.

➤ **To insert an identifier before inline responses**

1. On the **Personal Stationery** page of the **Signatures and Stationery** dialog box, in the **Replying or forwarding messages** area, select the **Mark my comments with** check box.

Or

On the **Mail** page of the **Outlook Options** dialog box, in the **Replies and forwards** section, select the **Preface comments with** check box.

2. In the corresponding text box, enter the text that will identify your responses.

➤ **To specify the text included in response messages**

→ On the **Mail** page of the **Outlook Options** dialog box, in the **Replies and forwards** section, click the message options you want for original content that is included in response messages, in the **When replying to a message** and **When forwarding a message** lists.

➤ **To have Outlook set the color of response text**

→ On the **Personal Stationery** page of the **Signatures and Stationery** dialog box, in the **Replying or forwarding messages** area, select the **Pick a new color when replying or forwarding** check box.

Create and assign automatic signatures

When you send an email message to someone, you will most likely "sign" the message by entering your name at the end of the message text. You can automatically insert your signature text in outgoing messages by creating an email signature and assigning it to your email account. Your email signature can include additional information (text and graphics) that you want to consistently provide to message recipients. If you have more than one email account set up in Outlook, you can instruct Outlook to insert a different signature in messages sent from each account.

> **See Also** For information about manually inserting email signatures in messages, see section 2.2, "Format messages."

➤ **To create and assign automatic signatures**

1. Open the **Outlook Options** dialog box.

2. In the **Compose messages** section of the **Mail** page, click the **Signatures** button.

3. On the **E-mail Signature** page of the **Signatures and Stationery** dialog box, click the **New** button.

4. In the **Type a name for this signature** box of the **New Signature** dialog box, enter a name that identifies the content or purpose of the signature, and then click **OK**.

5. In the **Edit signature** box, enter the signature text.

> **Tip** If you want to include your electronic business card as part of your signature, click the Business Card button. Then in the Insert Business Card dialog box, locate and click your name, and click OK.

6. Format the signature text by selecting the text and then using the formatting commands at the top of the **Edit signature** area.

> **Tip** Your signature will appear in email messages exactly as it does in the Edit Signature area.

7. In the **Choose default signature** area, select the email account to which you want to assign the signature. Then in the **New messages** list, click the signature name.

8. If you want to include the signature in message responses, in the **Replies/forwards** list, click the signature name.

9. Make any other changes you want, and then click **OK** in the **Signatures and Stationery** dialog box and in the **Outlook Options** dialog box.

Configure options for multiple accounts

You can add multiple email accounts of any type to your Outlook profile, either during setup or at any time thereafter. Outlook creates an Outlook data file for each email account and displays the account folders for each mailbox in the Folder Pane. You can manage each account separately by selecting the account in the Backstage view.

If you configure Outlook to connect to multiple email accounts, or if you have been delegated control of another account, you need to ensure that outgoing messages are sent from the correct account. By default, Outlook assumes that you intend to send a message from the account you're currently working in. If you begin composing a message while viewing the Inbox of your work account, for example, Outlook selects the work account as the message-sending account. If you reply to a message received by your personal account, Outlook selects the personal account as the message-sending account. You can change the sending account from within the message composition window.

> **See Also** For information about delegating access to accounts, see "Delegate access" in section 2.1, "Create messages."

➤ **To manage multiple accounts**

→ In the account list at the top of the **Info** page of the **Backstage** view, select the account you want to manage.

➤ **To specify the sending account**

→ If multiple accounts are configured in Outlook, click the **From** button in the message header, and then click the account from which you want to send the message.

→ If only one account is configured in Outlook, click the **From** button in the message header, and then click **Other E-mail Address**. In the **Send From Other E-mail Address** dialog box, enter the account from which you want to send the message in the **From** box.

Practice tasks

There are no practice files for these tasks.

- Create an automatic signature and assign it to appear in original messages only for your default email account.

- Configure Outlook to insert your initials between asterisks before comments that you insert in message responses.

- Configure your signature and response settings as you want them.

1.2 Automate Outlook

Automatically reply to messages

If your organization is running Microsoft Exchange Server, you can use the Automatic Replies feature to inform people who send you email messages of your availability. When you turn on the Automatic Replies feature, Outlook replies automatically to messages received from other people (but only to the first message from each person). You provide whatever textual information you want within the body of the automatic reply message (commonly referred to as an *out-of-office message*, or *OOF message*).

Tip You can configure rules to send automatic responses from accounts other than Exchange Server accounts. For more information, see "Automatically process messages" later in this section.

The functionality of the Automatic Replies feature is provided by Exchange Server, so the specific automatic reply options differ depending on what version of Exchange Server your organization is running. Regardless of which Exchange Server environment you're working in, this is a very useful feature. Your automatic reply message might also be displayed to co-workers in a MailTip at the top of messages they address to you, and displayed as part of your contact information in Microsoft Lync.

The purpose of the Automatic Replies feature is to provide standard information to message senders. When you're away from your computer, an automatic reply can set expectations for when a correspondent can expect a personal response from you. You don't have to be physically out of the office to use this feature; some people use it to let other people know when responses will be delayed for other reasons, such as when they are working on a project that will prevent them from responding promptly to messages, or to inform customers who might be in different time zones of their standard working hours.

In addition to having Outlook send automatic replies, you can have it process messages that arrive while you are out of the office by using rules that are in effect only when the Automatic Replies feature is on.

The Automatic Replies feature is off until you explicitly turn it on; it does not coordinate with your free/busy information in the Calendar module.

When you are using an Exchange account, you can do the following when configuring Automatic Replies:

- You can create two auto-reply messages—one that Outlook sends only to people in your organization (on the same domain) and another sent either to everyone else or only to the people in your primary address book.

  When you have separate internal and external messages, you can distinguish the information made available to co-workers, to friends and business contacts, and to the general public (including senders of spam). For example, you might include your itinerary and mobile phone number only in an internal automatic reply, include your return date in a reply to your contacts, and not send any reply to other people.

- You can specify the font, size, and color of automatic reply message text and apply bold, italic, or underline formatting.

- You can format paragraphs as bulleted or numbered lists and control the indent level.

- You can specify start and end dates and times for your automatic reply message so that you don't have to remember to turn off Automatic Replies.

➤ **To turn on automatic replies**

1. On the **Info** page of the **Backstage** view, click the **Automatic Replies** button.

2. In the **Automatic Replies** dialog box, on the **Inside My Organization** page, click the **Send automatic replies** option.

3. Select the **Only send during this time range** check box.

4. Set the **Start time** to the date and time when you want to start sending automatic replies, and the **End time** to the date and time you want to stop.

5. In the content pane, enter and format the message you want to send to internal recipients.

6. On the **Outside My Organization** page, select the **Auto-reply to people outside my organization** check box.

7. If you want to restrict automatic replies to only email messages that are in your Contacts address book, click the **My Contacts only** option.

8. In the content pane, enter and format the message you want to send to external recipients.

9. In the **Automatic Replies** dialog box, click **OK**.

Automatically process messages

You can have Outlook evaluate your incoming or outgoing email messages and take various actions with them based on sets of instructions you set up, called *rules*. You can create rules based on different message criteria, such as the message sender, message recipients, message content, attachments, and importance. By using rules, you can have Outlook move, copy, delete, forward, redirect, reply to, or otherwise process messages based on the criteria you specify. You can choose from a collection of standard rules or create your own from scratch.

If you have an Exchange Server account, you can set up rules that are applied to messages as they are received or processed by your Exchange server, and rules that go into effect only when you indicate that you are unavailable, by setting up an Automatic Reply. Whether or not you have an Exchange account, you can set up rules that are applied to messages stored on your computer.

You can base a rule on one of the 11 templates provided by Outlook, start from a blank rule, or copy and modify an existing rule.

Separately from the Outlook rules that you run manually or automatically, you can set up rules that run only when the Automatic Replies feature is active. The Automatic Reply rules are built on a different set of criteria than standard Outlook rules; you can choose from a limited number of conditions, and you can't specify exceptions.

➤ **To create a rule from scratch**

1. On the **Info** page of the **Backstage** view, click the **Manage Rules & Alerts** button.

2. On the **E-mail Rules** page of the **Rules and Alerts** dialog box, click **New Rule**.

3. In the **Rules Wizard**, do one of the following, and then click **Next**:

   ○ In the **Stay Organized** or **Stay Up to Date** section of the **Select a template** list, click the template from which you want to build the new rule.

   ○ In the **Start from a blank rule** section of the **Select a template** list, click the type of message you want the rule to process.

4. In the **Select condition(s)** list, select the check box for each of the conditions that will identify messages to be processed by the rule. In the **Edit the rule description** area, click each underlined word or phrase, and replace it with a criterion that identifies the target messages. Then click **Next**.

5. In the **Select action(s)** list, select the check box for each of the actions you want Outlook to perform. Specify the criteria for the underlined words or phrases. Then click **Next**.

6. In the **Select exception(s)** list, select the check box for any condition that will identify messages to exclude from the rule action. Specify the criteria for the underlined words or phrases. Then click **Next**.

7. Specify a name for the new rule, do any of the following, and then click **Finish**:

   ○ Select the **Run this rule now on messages already in "Inbox"** check box.

   ○ Select the **Turn on this rule** check box.

➤ **To modify an existing rule**

1. Open the **Rules and Alerts** dialog box. On the **E-mail Rules** page, in the **Rule** list, click the name of the rule you want to modify (do not select its check box). Click **Change Rule**, and then click **Edit Rule Settings**.

2. In the **Rules** wizard, modify the rule as necessary.

➤ **To create a new rule based on an existing rule**

1. Open the **Rules and Alerts** dialog box. On the **E-mail Rules** page, in the **Rule** list, click the name of the rule you want to use as the basis for the new rule. Then click **Copy**.

2. In the **Copy rule to** dialog box, if the **Folder** list includes multiple accounts or sets of accounts, click the account or set of accounts to which you want the rule to apply. Then click **OK**.

3. On the **E-mail Rules** page, with the copy selected, click **Change Rule**, and then click **Edit Rule Settings**.

4. In the **Rules** wizard, modify the rule as necessary, and specify a unique name for the rule on the final page of the wizard.

➤ **To apply a rule to a specific account or set of accounts**

1. In the **Rules and Alerts** dialog box, click the name of the rule for which you want to specify an account or set of accounts.

2. In the **Apply changes to this folder** list, click the account or set of accounts to which you want to apply the rule.

> **Tip** The Apply Changes To This Folder list is present only when Outlook is configured to connect to multiple Exchange accounts.

➤ **To run a rule on existing messages**

1. Open the **Rules and Alerts** dialog box. On the **E-mail Rules** page, click **Run Rules Now**.

2. In the **Run Rules Now** dialog box, select the check box of each rule you want to run, select the folder or folders and type of messages on which you want to run the rule or rules, and then click **Run Now**.

➤ **To delete a rule**

1. Open the **Rules and Alerts** dialog box. On the **E-mail Rules** page, in the **Rule** list, click the name of the rule you want to delete, and then click **Delete**.

2. In the **Microsoft Outlook** dialog box that appears, click **Yes**.

➤ **To create a rule that runs only when you are out of the office**

1. On the **Info** page of the **Backstage** view, click the **Automatic Replies** button.

2. In the **Automatic Replies** dialog box, click **Rules**.

3. In the **Automatic Reply Rules** dialog box, click **Add Rule**.

4. In the **When a message arrives that meets the following conditions** area of the **Edit Rule** dialog box, specify the conditions that define messages to be processed by the rule.

5. To specify additional conditions such as message size, receipt date, importance, and sensitivity, click **Advanced** and, in the **Advanced** dialog box, specify the conditions, and then click **OK**.

6. In the **Perform these actions** area of the **Edit Rule** dialog box, specify the actions to be performed by the rule.

7. Click **OK** in each of the three open dialog boxes (**Edit Rule**, **Automatic Reply Rules**, and **Automatic Replies**).

➤ **To specify rules to run while Automatic Replies are turned on**

1. On the **Info** page of the **Backstage** view, click the **Automatic Replies** button.

2. In the **Automatic Replies** dialog box, click **Rules**.

3. In the **Automatic Reply Rules** dialog box, select the check box for each rule you want to run, and clear the check box for each rule you don't want to run during the current out-of-office period. Then click **OK** in the **Automatic Reply Rules** and **Automatic Replies** dialog boxes.

Create and manage Quick Steps

With the Quick Steps feature, you can perform multiple processes on one or more email messages with only one click. For example, you can reply to an email message and delete the original message, or flag a message for follow-up and move it to a specific folder. Quick Steps are somewhat like rules, but you must initiate them manually.

A default Outlook installation includes these five Quick Steps:

- **Move to** Moves the selected message to a folder that you specify the first time you use the Quick Step and marks the message as read. After you specify the folder, the Quick Step name changes to include the folder name.

- **To Manager** Forwards the selected message to a person or people you specify the first time you use the Quick Step. You can edit the Quick Step to include Cc and Bcc recipients, a specific message subject, a follow-up flag, a level of importance, and specific message text, and to send the message one minute after you click the Quick Step command.

- **Team Email** Creates a message to a person or people you specify the first time you use the Quick Step. You can edit the Quick Step to include Cc and Bcc recipients, a specific message subject, a follow-up flag, a level of importance, and specific message text, and to send the message one minute after you click the Quick Step command.

- **Done** Moves the selected message to a folder that you specify the first time you use the Quick Step, marks the message as read, and marks the message as complete so that a check mark is displayed in the follow-up flag location.

- **Reply & Delete** Creates a response to the original message sender and immediately deletes the original message.

> **Troubleshooting** The Reply & Delete Quick Step deletes the original message before you send the reply. If you close the response message composition window without sending it, the original message will no longer be in your Inbox. If you want to respond to the original message, you first need to retrieve it from your Deleted Items folder.

Quick Steps are available from the Quick Steps group on the Home tab of the Mail module, and from the shortcut menu that appears when you right-click a message or group of messages.

For each of the built-in Quick Steps, you can change its name; edit, add, and remove actions; and specify tooltip text that appears when you point to the Quick Step in the Quick Steps gallery.

You can create your own Quick Steps that include any combination of up to 12 actions. You can base a new Quick Step on a standard set of actions or an existing Quick Step, or create it from scratch. You can assign shortcut keys (Ctrl+Shift+1 through Ctrl+Shift+9) to up to nine Quick Steps.

> **Tip** The Quick Steps feature is available only in the Mail module. If you connect to multiple accounts, the Quick Steps in each Mail module are specific to that account.

➤ **To set up and use an existing Quick Step**

1. On the **Home** tab, in the **Quick Steps** gallery, click the Quick Step you want to perform.

2. In the **First Time Setup** dialog box, provide the information required for the selected command, and then click **Save**.

   Or

   In the **First Time Setup** dialog box, provide the information required for the selected command, click **Options**, and then follow the instructions for changing the properties of an existing Quick Step.

➤ **To perform an existing Quick Step**

1. Select a message or group of messages.

2. On the **Home** tab, in the **Quick Steps** gallery, click the Quick Step you want to perform.

   Or

   Right-click the selection, point to **Quick Steps**, and then click the Quick Step you want to perform.

➤ **To view the properties of an existing Quick Step**

1. On the **Home** tab, click the **Quick Steps** dialog box launcher.

2. In the **Manage Quick Steps** dialog box, in the **Quick step** list, click the Quick Step you want to view.

➤ **To change the properties of an existing Quick Step**

1. In the **Quick Steps** gallery, right-click the Quick Step you want to modify, and then click **Edit <Quick Step name>**.

Or

On the **Home** tab, click the **Quick Steps** dialog box launcher. In the **Manage Quick Steps** dialog box, click the Quick Step you want to modify, and then click **Edit**.

2. In the **Edit Quick Step** dialog box, do any of the following, and then click **Save**:

- ○ To rename the Quick Step, replace the text in the **Name** box.

- ○ To replace an action, in the **Actions** list, click the existing action, and then click the replacement action. Supply any secondary information necessary for the replacement action.

- ○ To add an action, click the **Add Action** button. Click **Choose an Action**, and then click the action you want to add. Supply any secondary information necessary for the new action.

- ○ To assign a shortcut key combination to the Quick Step, in the **Shortcut key** list, click the key combination you want.

- ○ To change the message that appears when you point to the Quick Step, edit the text in the **Tooltip text** box.

➤ **To create a Quick Step**

1. In the **Quick Steps** gallery, click **Create New** to begin creating a custom Quick Step.

Or

Expand the **Quick Steps** gallery, click **New Quick Step**, and then click the basic action set you want the Quick Step to perform, or click **Custom**.

Or

Click the **Quick Steps** dialog box launcher. In the **Manage Quick Steps** dialog box, do one of the following:

- ○ Click **New**. Then click the basic action set you want the Quick Step to perform, or click **Custom**.

- ○ In the **Quick step** list, click an existing Quick Step on which you want to base the new Quick Step, and then click **Duplicate**.

2. In the **First Time Setup** or **Edit Quick Step** dialog box, provide the necessary information, and then click **Finish**.

➤ **To reset a built-in Quick Step**

1. On the **Home** tab, click the **Quick Steps** dialog box launcher.

2. In the **Manage Quick Steps** dialog box, in the **Quick step** list, click the Quick Step you want to reset.

3. Click **Reset to Defaults**, and then click **Yes** in the **Microsoft Outlook** dialog box that opens.

➤ **To delete a Quick Step**

→ In the **Quick Steps** gallery, right-click the Quick Step, and then click **Delete**.

→ Click the **Quick Steps** dialog box launcher. In the **Manage Quick Steps** dialog box, click the Quick Step you want to delete, and then click **Delete**.

Practice tasks

There are no practice files for these tasks.

- Create a rule that assigns all incoming messages from your manager to the Red category, or to another category of your choosing. Run the rule on your Inbox.

- Set up the built-in *Team E-mail* Quick Step to send a message with the subject *MOS Certification Information* to you and two other people. Specify that the message body should be prefilled with the text *New information about MOS Certification*.

- Create a Quick Step named *Categorize MOS* that does the following:
  - Assigns the message to a category named *MOS Study Guide*. (Create the category during the process of creating the Quick Step.)
  - Creates a task containing the text of the message.

- Use the *Team E-mail* Quick Step to create a message. Replace the built-in message body content with the text *I'm testing the Outlook 2013 Quick Step feature; please reply to this message.* Then send the message.

- After you receive the two responses to the *MOS Certification Information* message, run the *Categorize MOS* Quick Step on the two messages simultaneously.

- Delete the rule and the *Categorize MOS* Quick Step, and then reset the properties of the *Team E-mail* Quick Step.

1.3 Print and save information in Outlook

View and save messages and attachments

You can view message attachments in several ways:

- You can preview certain types of attachments (including Word documents, Excel workbooks, PowerPoint presentations, and PDF files) directly in the Reading Pane.

  When you click the attachment, the message text is replaced by a preview of the attachment contents, and the Attachments tool tab appears on the ribbon.

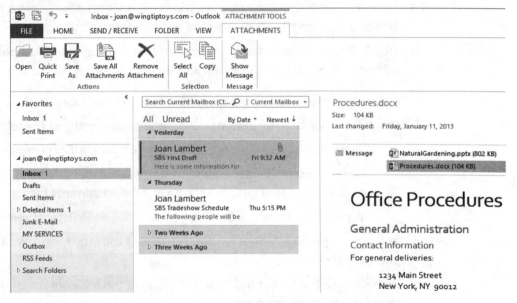

- You can open the attachment in the program assigned to that file type.

- You can save the attachment to your hard disk and open it from there. This strategy is recommended if you suspect an attachment might contain a virus because you can scan the file for viruses before opening it (provided that you have a virus scanning program installed).

If you want to save messages outside of Outlook, you can save either individual messages or entire folders of messages. Individual messages can be saved in several formats, including as Outlook message files, text files, and HTML files. Folders can be saved as Outlook data files, which can then be opened from any Outlook installation.

➤ **To preview message attachments**

→ In the **Reading Pane**, click the attachment (one time) in the message header.

→ To redisplay the message content, click the **Message** button that appears to the left of the attachments in the message header.

➤ **To open message attachments**

→ In the **Reading Pane** or in an open message window, double-click the attachment in the message header.

➤ **To save message attachments to Outlook**

→ To add a contact record or business card to your primary address book, drag the attachment from the email message to the **Contacts** button on the **Navigation Bar**.

→ To add a contact record or business card to a secondary address book, display the address book in the **Folder Pane**, and then drag the attachment to that folder.

➤ **To save message attachments to a file storage location**

1. Open the **Save All Attachments** dialog box by doing any of the following:

   o Right-click any attachment, and then click **Save All Attachments**.

   o In the message header, click a message attachment. Then on the **Attachments** tool tab, click the **Save All Attachments** button.

   o In the left pane of the **Backstage** view, click **Save Attachments**.

2. In the **Save All Attachments** dialog box, select the attachments you want to save, and then click **OK**.

3. In the **Save Attachment** dialog box, browse to the folder in which you want to save the files, and then click **Save**.

➤ **To save messages as files**

1. In the **Backstage** view of the message reading window, click **Save As**.

2. In the **Save As** dialog box, browse to the folder in which you want to save the message.

3. In the **Save as type** list, click the format in which you want to save the message.

4. If you want to change the name of the message file, replace the message subject in the **File name** box.

5. In the **Save As** dialog box, click **Save**.

➤ **To export messages to an Outlook data file**

1. On the **Open & Export** page of the **Backstage** view, click **Import/Export** to start the **Import and Export Wizard**.

2. In the **Choose an action to perform** list, click **Export to a file**, and then click **Next**.

3. In the **Create a file of type** list, click **Outlook Data File (.pst)**, and then click **Next**.

4. In the **Select the folder to export from** list, click the folder from which you want to export messages.

5. If you want to export only some of the messages from the folder, click **Filter** to open the **Filter** dialog box, filter the folder to display only the messages you want to export, and then click **OK**.

6. In the **Export Outlook Data File** wizard, click **Next**.

7. To the right of the **Save exported file as** box, click the **Browse** button. In the **Open Outlook Data Files** dialog box, browse to the folder in which you want to save the .pst file. Enter a name for the exported file in the **File name** box, click **OK**, and then click **Next**.

> **Tip** If other data files exist in the Open Outlook Data Files dialog box, the File Name box will automatically display the name of an existing file. You must replace that file name or the previous file will be overwritten.

8. On the wizard's last page, click **Finish**.

9. In the **Create Outlook Data File** dialog box, if you want to password-protect the file, enter a password in the **Password** and **Verify Password** boxes. Then click **OK** to create the file.

Print Outlook items

In Outlook 2013, you can print any item from the content pane or from the item window.

You can print a list of the email messages in your Inbox or print one or more individual email messages. Outlook prints the message as shown on the screen, including font and paragraph formats. You can add information such as page headers and footers.

When printing a calendar, the amount of detail that appears depends on the time period you print and the print style you choose.

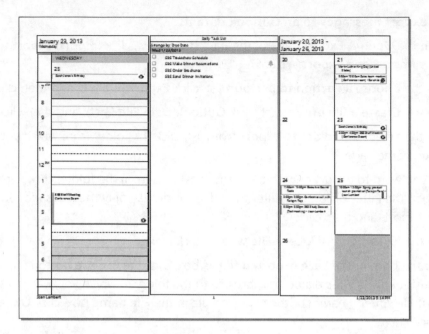

Outlook offers several built-in print styles for calendars, and you can create others if you want. The available print styles vary based on what view you're in when you choose the Print command. The default print styles include:

- **Daily Style** Prints the selected date range with one day per page. Printed elements include the date, day, TaskPad, reference calendar for the current month, and an area for notes.

- **Weekly Agenda Style** Prints the selected date range with one calendar week per page, including reference calendars for the selected and following month.

- **Weekly Calendar Style** Prints the selected date range with one calendar week per page. Each page includes date range and time increments, reference calendars for the selected and following month, and TaskPad.

- **Monthly Style** Prints a page for each month in the selected date range. Each page includes the selected month with a few days showing from the previous and subsequent months, along with reference calendars for the selected and following month.

- **Tri-fold Style** Prints a page for each day in the selected date range. Each page includes the daily schedule, weekly schedule, and TaskPad.

- **Calendar Details Style** Lists your appointments for the selected date range, in addition to the accompanying appointment details.

You can select the date or range of dates to be printed and modify the page setup options to fit your needs.

You can print an address book or individual contact records, either on paper or to an electronic file (such as a PDF file or an XPS file), from any address book view.

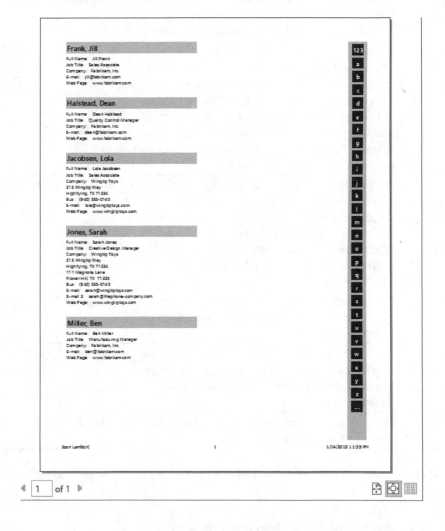

◀ | 1 | of 1 ▶

Depending on the view, Outlook offers a variety of print styles, such as those described in the following table.

Style	Description	Available in these views
Card	Contact information displayed alphabetically in two columns. Letter graphics appear at the top of each page and the beginning of each letter group.	Business Card, Card, People
Small Booklet	Contact information displayed alphabetically in one column. Formatted to print eight numbered pages per sheet. Letter graphics appear at the top of each page and the beginning of each letter group, and a contact index at the side of each page indicates the position of that page's entries in the alphabet.	Business Card, Card, People
Medium Booklet	Contact information displayed alphabetically in one column. Formatted to print four numbered pages per sheet. Letter graphics appear at the top of each page and the beginning of each letter group, and a contact index at the side of each page indicates the position of that page's entries in the alphabet.	Business Card, Card, People
Memo	Contact information displayed under a memo-like header that contains your name. One record per sheet.	Business Card, Card, People
Phone Directory	Contact names and phone numbers displayed in two columns. Letter graphics appear at the top of each page and the beginning of each letter group.	Business Card, Card, People
Table	Contact information displayed in a table that matches the on-screen layout.	Phone, List

You can customize the layout of most of the default print styles, and save the modified print styles.

➤ **To print the default view of an individual item**

➜ Right-click the item, and then click **Quick Print**.

➤ **To print an individual item**

1. In the item window, display the **Print** page of the **Backstage** view.

2. Specify the print options and settings you want, and then click the **Print** button.

➤ **To print multiple items**

1. In the content pane, select the items you want to print.

2. On the **Print** page of the **Backstage** view, specify the print options and settings you want, and then click **Print**.

➤ **To print a list view of all messages in a folder**

→ On the **Print** page of the program window **Backstage** view, in the **Settings** section, click **Table Style**, and then click the **Print** button.

➤ **To print an email message and its attachments**

1. On the **Print** page of the **Backstage** view, click the **Print Options** button.

2. In the **Print** dialog box, select the **Print attached files** check box. Then click **Print**.

➤ **To print a message attachment**

1. In the **Reading Pane** or message window, select the attachments you want to print.

2. On the **Attachments** tool tab, in the **Actions** group, click the **Quick Print** button.

➤ **To print a calendar**

1. In the Calendar module, on the **Print** page of the **Backstage** view, click the **Print Options** button.

2. In the **Print** dialog box, do the following:

    a. In the **Print style** list, click the print style you want.

    b. In the **Print range** section, specify the date range you want to print.

    c. If you want to exclude private appointments from the printed calendar, select the **Hide details of private appointments** check box.

3. In the **Print** dialog box, click the **Preview** button.

4. On the **Print** page of the **Backstage** view, click the **Print** button.

➤ **To print multiple contact records**

1. In the People module, if you want to print only specific contact records, select those contact records.

2. On the **Print** page of the **Backstage** view, click the **Print Options** button.

3. In the **Print** dialog box, do the following:

    a. In the **Print style** list, click the print style you want.

    b. In the **Print range** section, click **All items** or **Only selected items**.

4. In the **Print** dialog box, click the **Preview** button.

5. On the **Print** page of the **Backstage** view, click the **Print** button.

➤ **To print tasks**

1. In the Tasks module, if you want to print only specific task items and flagged items, select those items.

2. On the **Print** page of the **Backstage** view, click the **Print Options** button.

3. In the **Print** dialog box, do the following:

    a. In the **Print style** list, click the print style you want.

    b. In the **Print options** section, if you want to print files that are attached to the task items or flagged items, select the **Print attached files** check box.

4. In the **Print** dialog box, click the **Preview** button.

5. On the **Print** page of the **Backstage** view, click the **Print** button.

Practice tasks

There are no practice files for these tasks.

- In your Inbox, select two email messages that have attachments. In one operation, print both messages and their attachments.

- Print your calendar for the next three days so that the daily schedule for each day appears on its own page with space for a task list.

- Select four contact records and print a list of the names and phone numbers.

- Print a table-style list of all your current tasks.

1.4 Search in Outlook

Search for items

The Instant Search feature of Outlook 2013 makes it easy to find a specific Outlook item based on any text within the item or any attribute, such as the category assigned to it. With this very powerful search engine, you can find any message containing a specified search term, whether the term appears in the item header, in the item content, or in a message attachment.

Although you can use Instant Search to locate calendar items, contact records, and tasks, you will most often use it to locate messages in your Inbox and other mail folders. Regardless of the module you're searching from, you can search a specific folder, all folders containing items of that type, or all of Outlook. As you enter a search term, Outlook filters out all messages that don't match, displays only those items containing the characters you enter, and highlights the search term in the displayed results, making it easy to find exactly what you're looking for.

Outlook first displays up to 30 recent results. Clicking the More link at the bottom of the list or the Include Older Results button in the Results group on the Search tool tab displays additional results within the selected search scope. In the lower-left corner of the program window, the status bar displays the number of items included in the search results.

You can narrow the results by expanding the search term or by specifying other search criteria, such as the sender, the recipient (whether the message was addressed or only copied to you), a category assigned to the item, or whether the message contains attachments.

The Search tool tab appears when you activate the Search box in any Outlook module. You can enter search terms into the Search box and refine your search by using the commands on the Search tool tab.

When searching any folder, you can use the commands on the Search tool tab to set the scope of the search and to more closely define the search specifications. You can also return to the results of previous searches.

The buttons available in the Scope and Refine groups vary based on the type of folder you're searching. The Scope group always offers the options of the current folder, all subfolders, all folders of the current type, and all Outlook items. The commands in the Refine group change to reflect common properties of items stored in the current folder type. The most common properties are shown as buttons in the Refine group; additional properties are available for selection from the More list.

Unless you specify otherwise, the search results include only the contents of the displayed folder, not any of its subfolders or any other folders. However, you can choose to search all similar folders or all Outlook items. If you search more than one folder, Outlook displays the search results grouped by the folder in which they appear.

You can open, delete, and process an item from the search results as you would from any other location. However, if you change an item so that it no longer fits the search criteria, the item no longer appears in the search results.

➤ **To search Outlook items in a specific folder**

1. In the **Search** box at the top of the content pane, enter the search term.
2. On the **Search** tool tab, in the **Refine** group, click buttons to specify additional search criteria.

➤ **To change the scope of the search operation**

→ On the **Search** tool tab, in the **Scope** group, click the **All Items** button for the type of item contained in the current folder (for example, **All Mail Items** or **All Calendar Items**) to search all items of that type.

→ On the **Search** tool tab, in the **Scope** group, click the **All Subfolders** button to include subfolders of the current folder in the search.

→ On the **Search** tool tab, in the **Scope** group, click the **All Outlook Items** button to include messages, appointments, contact records, tasks, notes, and journal entries in the search.

> **Tip** The All Items and All Outlook Items searches include all accounts configured in your Outlook installation.

➤ **To return to the original content view**

→ On the **Search** tool tab, in the **Close** group, click the **Close Search** button.

→ Click any folder in the **Folder Pane**.

➤ **To quickly return to previous search results**

1. Click in the **Search** box at the top of the content pane to display the **Search** tool tab.

2. On the **Search** tab, in the **Options** group, click the **Recent Searches** button, and then click the search you want to repeat.

Use Search Folders

A Search Folder displays all the messages in your mailbox that match a specific set of search criteria, no matter which folders the messages are actually stored in. When you create a Search Folder, it becomes part of your mailbox and is kept up to date. The Search Folder module is located in the Folder Pane, within your top-level mailbox, at the same level as the Inbox.

By default, Outlook 2013 includes one standard Search Folder: Unread Mail. (If your environment includes Microsoft Lync, you might also have Search Folders for Missed Calls and Missed Conversations.) If you want quick access to messages that fit a specific set of criteria, you can create a custom Search Folder. Search Folder categories include Reading Mail, Mail From People And Lists, Organizing Mail, and Custom.

Outlook automatically keeps Search Folder contents up to date. The names of folders containing unread or flagged items are bold, with the number of unread items after the folder name. The names of folders whose contents are not up to date are italic.

Each message in your mailbox is stored in only one folder (such as your Inbox), but it might appear in multiple Search Folders. Changing or deleting a message in a Search Folder changes or deletes the message in the folder in which it is stored.

➤ **To create Search Folders**

1. Display any mail folder.

2. On the **Folder** tab, in the **New** group, click **New Search Folder** to open the **New Search Folder** dialog box.

   Or

   In the **Folder List**, within the mailbox for which you want to create the Search Folder, click **Search Folders**, and then click **New Search Folder**.

   Or

   Press **Ctrl+Shift+P**.

3. In the **New Search Folder** dialog box, click the type of Search Folder you want to create, provide the search criteria that define the Search Folder contents, and then click **OK**.

➤ **To modify criteria for an existing Search Folder**

1. Right-click the folder, and then click **Customize This Search Folder**.

2. Modify the Search Folder name or criteria, and then click **OK**.

➤ **To update a Search Folder**

→ In the **Folder List**, click the folder name.

Practice tasks

There are no practice files for these tasks.

- Use the Instant Search feature to locate a specific message in your Inbox.
- Without changing the search term, expand the search to include all Outlook items.
- Search all Outlook items for anything related to a specific person, such as your manager.
- Search all Outlook items for anything you have assigned to a specific category, such as the Management category. Then search for all items that have attachments.
- Create a Search Folder containing all the messages in your Inbox (not your mailbox) from a specific person, such as your manager.

Objective review

Before finishing this chapter, ensure that you have mastered the following skills:

1.1 Customize Outlook settings

1.2 Automate Outlook

1.3 Print and save information in Outlook

1.4 Search in Outlook

2 Manage messages

The skills tested in this section of the Microsoft Office Specialist exam for Microsoft Outlook 2013 relate to managing messages. Specifically, the following objectives are associated with this set of skills:

2.1 Create messages

2.2 Format messages

2.3 Organize and manage messages

Although Microsoft Outlook 2013 is an excellent tool for managing your schedule, contact records, and task lists, the primary reason most people use Outlook is to send and receive email messages. Over the past decade, email (short for *electronic mail*) has become an accepted and even required form of business communication. And of course, many people use email to keep in touch with friends and family, either from work or from home. Outlook makes it easy to connect to multiple email accounts, either on a business network or over the Internet, and provides all the tools you need to send, respond to, organize, filter, sort, find, and otherwise manage email messages.

Messages composed in and sent from Outlook 2013 don't have to consist only of plain text. They can contain diagrams and graphics and can be visually enhanced by a judicious use of colors, fonts, and backgrounds. For more formal messages, you can attach a signature that includes your contact information, in addition to graphics such as a photograph or logo.

Even if you use Outlook only for sending and receiving email messages, you can rapidly build up a mass of messages that make it difficult to locate information. Fortunately, Outlook is designed to act as a complete information-management system; it provides many simple yet useful features that you can use to organize messages and other Outlook items and to quickly find information you need.

Outlook 2013 automatically handles certain types of organization for you. You can organize items in Outlook by storing related items in folders and by assigning color categories to related items of all types. Outlook makes it easy to follow related messages from multiple people by displaying the messages in Conversation view.

This chapter guides you in studying ways of creating, formatting, organizing, and managing messages.

> **Practice Files** To complete the practice tasks in this chapter, you need the practice files contained in the MOSOutlook2013\Objective2 practice file folder. For more information, see "Download the practice files" in this book's Introduction.

2.1 Create messages

Create and send messages

You can send a message from any account for which you have permission. Valid sending accounts include those that are configured on your computer and other accounts for which you have been delegated permission.

> **See Also** For information about delegating permission to accounts, see "Delegate access" later in this section. For information about sending from alternative accounts, see "Configure options for multiple accounts" in section 1.1, "Customize Outlook settings."

In addition to the To and Cc fields, which are displayed by default in the message composition window, you can display the From field and the Bcc field. When you display or hide these optional message header fields in an individual message, Outlook retains the setting for all message composition windows.

A convenient way to distribute a file (such as a Microsoft Word document, Excel work-book, PowerPoint presentation, or picture) is by attaching the file to an email message. Message recipients can preview or open the file from the Reading Pane, open it from the message window, forward it to other people, or save it to their computers.

You can also attach Outlook items, such as other messages, calendar items, contact records, notes, and tasks, to outgoing messages. Recipients can save attached items in their own Outlook installations.

➤ **To create an original message**

→ In the Mail module, on the **Home** tab, in the **New** group, click the **New Email** button.

→ In the Mail module, press **Ctrl+N**.

→ In any module, on the **Home** tab, in the **New** group, click the **New Items** button, and then click **E-mail Message**.

→ In any module, press **Ctrl+Shift+M**.

➤ **To display optional address fields**

→ On the **Options** tab of the message window, in the **Show Fields** group, click the **Bcc** button.

➤ **To attach one or more files to a message**

→ Drag the file or files you want to attach to the message from File Explorer into the message area of the message window.

> **Tip** In Windows 8, File Explorer has replaced Windows Explorer. Throughout this book, we refer to this utility by its Windows 8 name. If your computer is running Windows 7 or an earlier version of Windows, use Windows Explorer instead.

Or

1. On the **Message** tab or **Insert** tab of the message window, in the **Include** group, click the **Attach File** button.

2. In the **Insert File** dialog box, locate and click the first file you want to attach. To attach multiple files, press the **Ctrl** key and click the additional files.

3. In the **Insert File** dialog box, click **Insert**.

➤ **To attach an Outlook item to a message**

→ Drag the item you want to attach to the message from the content pane into the message area of the message window.

Or

1. On the **Message** tab of the message window, in the **Include** group, click the **Attach Item** button, and then click **Outlook Item**.

2. In the **Insert Item** dialog box, locate and click the item you want to attach.

3. With **Attachment** selected in the **Insert as** area, click **OK**.

Configure message options

When you send a message, you can include visual indicators of the importance, sensitivity, or subject category of a message or other Outlook item, flag a message for follow-up, restrict other people from changing or forwarding message content, provide a simple feedback mechanism in the form of voting buttons, and specify message delivery options to fit your needs.

Message settings and delivery options

Common message settings and delivery options include the following:

- **Flags and reminders** You can place an outgoing message on your task list, add an informational reminder to it, or set a reminder to appear at a certain time and date, for yourself and for message recipients.

- **Importance** You can indicate the urgency of a message by setting its importance to High or Low. A corresponding banner appears in the message header and, if the Importance field is included in the view, an importance icon appears in the Inbox or other message folder.

- **Sensitivity** You can indicate that a message should be kept private by setting its sensitivity to Confidential, Personal, or Private. No indicator appears in the message folder, but a banner appears in the message header to indicate a sensitivity level other than Normal.

- **Security** If you have a digital ID, you can digitally sign the message; or you can encrypt the contents of the message.

- **Voting options** If you and your message recipients have Microsoft Exchange Server accounts, you can add voting buttons to your messages so that recipients can quickly select from multiple-choice response options.

- **Tracking options** You can track messages by requesting delivery receipts and read receipts. These receipts are messages automatically generated by the recipient's email server when it delivers the message to the recipient and when the recipient opens the message.

- **Delivery options** You can have reply messages delivered to an email address other than yours, specify a date and time for the message to be delivered and to expire, and set advanced attachment format and encoding options.

- **Categories** You can assign a message to a color category that will be visible to the recipient if he or she views the message in Outlook.

> **Tip** You can easily sort and group messages by any message settings by choosing that message setting in the Arrange By list.

The most commonly used options are available in the Tags group on the Message tab of the message window. You can access other options from the Properties dialog box, which you open by clicking the Tags dialog box launcher.

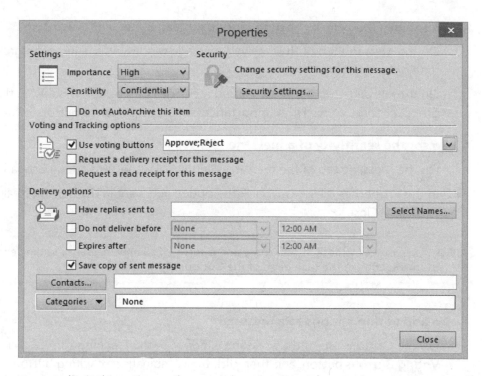

You can limit the actions other people can take with messages they receive from you by restricting the message permissions. For example, you can prevent recipients from forwarding or printing the message, copying the message content, or changing the content when they forward or reply to the message. (Restrictions apply also to message attachments.) Within a message window, permission options are available both on the Info page of the Backstage view and in the Permission group on the Options tab.

➤ **To designate a message as high or low priority**

→ On the **Message** tab of the message window, in the **Tags** group, click the **High Importance** or **Low Importance** button.

Or

1. On the **Message** tab of the message window, click the **Tags** dialog box launcher.

2. In the **Properties** dialog box, click the option you want in the **Importance** list, and then click **Close**.

➤ **To remove the priority setting from a message you are forwarding**

1. On the **Message** tab of the received message window, in the **Respond** group, click the **Forward** button.

2. On the **Message** tab of the forwarded message composition window, in the **Tags** group, click the active **High Importance** or **Low Importance** button to turn it off.

➤ **To set the sensitivity of a message**

1. On the **Message** tab of the message window, click the **Tags** dialog box launcher.

2. In the **Properties** dialog box, click the option you want in the **Sensitivity** list, and then click **Close**.

> **Tip** You can set the default sensitivity and priority of all new messages in the Send Messages section of the Mail page of the Outlook Options dialog box.

➤ **To add voting options to a message**

➜ On the **Options** tab of the message window, in the **Tracking** group, click the **Use Voting Buttons** button, and then click the combination of voting buttons you want.

Or

1. On the **Options** tab, click the **More Options** dialog box launcher.

Or

On the **Options** tab of the message window, in the **Tracking** group, click the **Use Voting Buttons** button, and then click **Custom**.

2. In the **Voting and Tracking options** area of the **Properties** dialog box, select the **Use voting buttons** check box.

3. In the **Use voting buttons** list, do one of the following:

○ Click the combination of voting buttons you want in the list.

○ Enter the voting button labels you want, separated by semicolons.

4. In the **Properties** dialog box, click **Close**.

➤ **To request a message receipt**

1. On the **Options** tab, click the **More Options** dialog box launcher.

2. In the **Voting and Tracking options** area of the **Properties** dialog box, do any of the following:

   ○ Select the **Request a delivery receipt for this message** check box to request notification when the message is delivered to the recipient's mailbox.

   ○ Select the **Request a read receipt for this message** check box to request notification when the message is marked as read.

3. In the **Properties** dialog box, click **Close**.

➤ **To schedule the delivery of a message**

1. On the **Options** tab, in the **More Options** group, click the **Delay Delivery** button.

   Or

   On the **Options** tab, click the **More Options** dialog box launcher.

2. In the **Delivery options** area of the **Properties** dialog box, click the date and time at which you want Outlook to send the message in the **Do not deliver before** lists.

3. In the **Properties** dialog box, click **Close**.

➤ **To set an expiration for a message**

1. On the **Options** tab, click the **More Options** dialog box launcher.

2. In the **Delivery options** area of the **Properties** dialog box, select the **Expires after** check box, and then click the date and time at which you want the message to expire in the **Expires after** lists.

3. In the **Properties** dialog box, click **Close**.

➤ **To direct responses to an alternative email address**

1. On the **Options** tab, in the **More Options** group, click the **Direct Replies To** button.

   Or

   On the **Options** tab, click the **More Options** dialog box launcher.

2. In the **Delivery options** area of the **Properties** dialog box, enter the email address to which you want responses to be delivered in the **Have replies sent to** box.

3. In the **Properties** dialog box, click **Close**.

Respond to messages

After you read a message, Outlook indicates its status as Read by removing the bold formatting and blue bar from the message header. You can change the read status of a message to provide visual cues or to affect the number that appears after the folder name in the Folder Pane.

You can respond to most email messages that you receive by clicking a response button either in the Reading Pane, in the Respond group on the Home tab of the program window, or in the Respond group on the Message tab of the message window.

The most standard response to a message is a reply. When you reply to a message, Outlook fills in one or more of the address boxes for you, as follows:

- **Reply** Creates an email message, addressed to only the original message sender, that contains the original message text.

- **Reply All** Creates an email message, addressed to the message sender and all recipients listed in the To and Cc boxes, that contains the original message text. The message is not addressed to recipients of blind courtesy copies (Bcc recipients).

- **Reply with Meeting** Creates a meeting invitation addressed to all message recipients. The message text is included in the meeting window content pane. Outlook suggests the current date and an upcoming half-hour time slot for the meeting.

Message replies include the original message header and text, preceded by a space in which you can respond. Replies do not include any attachments from the original message.

You can add, change, and delete recipients from any reply before sending it.

You can forward a received message to any email address (regardless of whether the recipient uses Outlook) provided the message was not sent with restricted permissions. Outlook 2013 has the following message-forwarding options:

- **Forward** Creates a new message that contains the text of the original, and retains any attachments from the original message.

- **Forward As Attachment** Creates a blank message that contains no text but includes the original message as an attachment. The original message text and any attachments are available to the new recipient when he or she opens the attached message.

When you forward a message, Outlook does not fill in the recipient boxes for you (the assumption being that you want to forward the message to someone who wasn't included on the original message).

➤ **To mark messages as read or unread**

1. Select the message or messages for which you want to change the status.
2. Right-click the selection, and then click **Mark as Read** or **Mark as Unread**.

➤ **To reply only to the message sender**

→ On the **Home** tab, in the **Respond** group, click the **Reply** button.

→ In the **Reading Pane**, in the message header, click the **Reply** button.

→ Press **Ctrl+R**.

➤ **To reply to all message recipients**

→ On the **Home** tab, in the **Respond** group, click the **Reply All** button.

→ In the **Reading Pane**, in the message header, click the **Reply All** button.

→ Press **Ctrl+Shift+R**.

➤ **To forward a message**

→ On the **Home** tab, in the **Respond** group, click the **Forward** button.

→ In the **Reading Pane**, in the message header, click the **Forward** button.

→ Press **Ctrl+F**.

➤ **To delete messages**

1. Select the message, messages, or conversation you want to delete.

2. Press the **Delete** key.

Or

On the **Home** tab, in the **Delete** group, click the **Delete** button.

3. If prompted to confirm the deletion, click **Yes**.

Delegate access

You can delegate control of one or more Outlook modules to a co-worker so that person can create messages, appointments, tasks, contact records, and notes, and respond to requests on your behalf.

When delegating access, you can assign specific permission levels for each module. Permission options include the following:

- **None** The delegate cannot read, create, or modify items in the module.

- **Reviewer** The delegate can read items in the module, but cannot create or modify items.

- **Author** The delegate can read and create items in the module, but cannot modify existing items.

- **Editor** The delegate can read, create, and modify items in the module.

When delegating permissions, the default settings give the delegate Editor permissions to the Calendar and Tasks modules only. However, you can also delegate permission to your Inbox, Contacts module, and Notes module.

Tip When you delegate permissions to your calendar, you can specify whether meeting requests are sent only to you, only to your delegates, or to both you and your delegates.

➤ **To delegate control of your account to another Outlook user**

1. On the **Info** page of the **Backstage** view, click **Account Settings**, and then click **Delegate Access**.

2. In the **Delegates** dialog box, click **Add**.

3. In the **Add Users** dialog box, click the person you want to delegate control to, click **Add**, and then click **OK**.

4. In the **Delegate Permissions** dialog box, set the permission level you want the delegate to have for each module.

5. If you want to inform your delegate about the permission he or she has to your account, select the **Automatically send a message...** check box.

6. If you want to allow your delegate to view details of items that you mark as private, select the **Delegate can see my private items** check box.

7. In the **Delegate Permissions** dialog box, click **OK**.

➤ **To modify delegation permissions**

1. On the **Info** page of the **Backstage** view, click **Account Settings**, and then click **Delegate Access**.

2. In the **Delegates** dialog box, select the delegate, and then click **Permissions**.

3. In the **Delegate Permissions** dialog box, set the permission level you want the delegate to have for each module, select any additional options, and then click **OK**.

➤ **To rescind a delegation**

1. On the **Info** page of the **Backstage** view, click **Account Settings**, and then click **Delegate Access**.

2. In the **Delegates** dialog box, select the delegate, click **Remove**, and then click **OK**.

Practice tasks

The practice files for these tasks are located in the MOSOutlook2013\Objective2 practice file folder. Save the results of the tasks in the same folder.

- Compose a message to yourself with the subject *MOS Sensitivity* and flag it as personal.

- Configure the message to expire in five minutes, and then send it.

- After the *MOS Sensitivity* message expires, mark it as unread.

- Send a message to yourself with the subject *MOS Secret* and flag it as both high priority and confidential.

- After you receive the *MOS Secret* message, forward it to yourself with a normal priority setting.

- Send a message to yourself with the subject *MOS Vote* that has *I Will*, *I Might*, and *I Will Not* voting buttons. Respond to the poll when you receive it.

- Create a message with the subject *MOS Files*. Attach the *Outlook_2-1a* document to the message. Use a different technique to attach the *Outlook_2-1b* presentation to the message. Then send the *MOS Files* message to yourself.

- When the *MOS Files* message arrives, preview the attached presentation in the Reading Pane. Then open the attached document in Word.

- Create a message with the subject *MOS Items*. Attach any contact record and any calendar item to the message. Then send the *MOS Items* message to yourself.

2.2 Format messages

Format text

You can manually format text in the content pane to differentiate it from your default font. The local formatting options available in Outlook 2013 are the same as those available in Word 2013, PowerPoint 2013, and other Office 2013 programs. You might already be familiar with the formatting options from working with those programs. Here's a quick review of the types of formatting changes you can make.

- **Font, size, and color** More than 220 fonts in a range of sizes and in a virtually unlimited selection of colors

- **Font style** Regular, bold, italic, or bold italic

- **Underline style and color** Plain, multiple, dotted, dashed, wavy, and many combinations thereof, in all colors

- **Effects** Strikethrough, superscript, subscript, shadow, outline, emboss, engrave, small caps, all caps, or hidden

- **Character spacing** Scale, spacing, position, and kerning

- **Paragraph attributes** Alignment, indentation, and spacing

- **Character and paragraph styles** Titles, headings, and purpose-specific font formatting (for example, for quotes and book titles)

➤ **To apply local formatting to selected text**

→ On the **Mini Toolbar**, click or select the formatting you want to apply.

→ In the **Basic Text** group the **Message** tab, or in the **Font** or **Paragraph** group on the **Format Text** tab, click or select the formatting option.

→ On the **Message** tab, click the **Basic Text** dialog box launcher. On the **Font** and **Advanced** pages of the **Font** dialog box, click or select the formatting you want to apply, and then click **OK**.

→ On the **Format Text** tab, click the **Font** dialog box launcher. In the **Font** dialog box, click or select the formatting you want to apply, and then click **OK**.

→ On the **Format Text** tab, click the **Paragraph** dialog box launcher. On the **Indents and Spacing** and **Line and Page Breaks** pages of the **Paragraph** dialog box, click or select the formatting you want to apply, and then click **OK**.

➤ **To apply existing formatting to other text**

1. In the message composition window, position the cursor in the formatted text or paragraph.

2. On the **Message** tab or **Format Text** tab, in the **Clipboard** group, click the **Format Painter** button to store the character and paragraph formatting of the selected text or active paragraph for a single use.

   Or

   In the **Clipboard** group, double-click the **Format Painter** button to store the formatting of the selected text or active paragraph for multiple uses.

3. Drag the paintbrush-shaped cursor across the text to which you want to apply the stored formatting.

4. If necessary, click the **Format Painter** button or press the **Esc** key to turn off the Format Painter tool.

> **Tip** When you are working with certain content elements such as tables and graphics, one or more tool tabs containing formatting commands specific to that element appear on the ribbon. You must select the element to access its formatting commands.

Apply themes and styles

You can change the appearance of the text in a message by applying either local formatting (character or paragraph attributes and styles that you apply directly to text) or global formatting (a theme that you apply to the entire document) in the same way that you would when working in a Word document or PowerPoint presentation.

> **Tip** You can set a default theme for new email messages from the Personal Stationery page of the Signatures And Stationery dialog box. For information, see section 1.1, "Customize Outlook settings."

Nine of the standard Microsoft Office 2013 themes (which are not the same as the email message themes you can select in the Theme Or Stationery dialog box) are available from the Themes gallery on the Options tab in a message composition window. Each theme controls the colors, fonts, and graphic effects used in the message.

The default theme for all email messages, Word documents, PowerPoint presentations, Excel workbooks, and other Office 2013 documents is the Office theme. If you don't apply another theme to your message, the colors, fonts, and effects in your message are controlled by the Office theme.

> ➤ **To apply a theme to an individual message**

> → In the message composition window, on the **Options** tab, in the **Themes** group, click the **Themes** button, and then click the theme you want to apply.

Apply styles

A style is a combination of character formatting and paragraph formatting that you can apply to selected text or the active paragraph with one click. You can use styles to format text in email messages in the same way that you do in Word documents.

> **Strategy** If the existing styles don't meet your needs, you can modify existing styles and create styles from scratch. Modifying and creating styles is beyond the scope of this exam.

➤ **To display the Styles pane**

→ In the message composition window, on the **Format Text** tab, click the **Styles** dialog box launcher.

➤ **To preview the effect of a style on selected text**

→ On the **Format Text** tab, in the **Quick Styles** gallery, point to the style.

➤ **To apply a style to selected text**

→ In the **Quick Styles** gallery or in the **Styles** pane, click the style.

Create hyperlinks

Outlook automatically converts URLs that you enter in a message content pane into hyperlinks that the recipient can click to display the webpage. You can manually create a hyperlink from any text or graphic to a heading or bookmark within the message or to an external file or webpage. You can also create a hyperlink that the recipient can click to create a new email message that already has the To and Subject fields populated.

➤ **To create a hyperlink to an existing file**

1. Select the text or graphic from which you want to link.

2. On the **Insert** tab, in the **Links** group, click the **Hyperlink** button.

3. In the **Insert Hyperlink** dialog box, in the **Link to** list, click **Existing File or Web Page**.

4. In the **Look in** area, browse to the file you want to link to.

   Or

   Click the **Browse for File** button and then, in the **Link to File** dialog box, browse to the file and click **Open**.

5. In the **Insert Hyperlink** dialog box, click **OK**.

➤ **To create a Word document and a hyperlink to it**

1. Select the text or graphic from which you want to link.

2. On the **Insert** tab, in the **Links** group, click the **Hyperlink** button.

3. In the **Insert Hyperlink** dialog box, in the **Link to** list, click **Create New Document**.

4. In the **Name of new document** box, enter a name for the document.

5. To create the document in a folder other than your Documents folder, click the **Change** button, browse to the folder in which you want to save the file, and then click **OK**.

6. In the **When to edit** area, do one of the following:

   ○ Click **Edit the new document later** to create a blank document.

   ○ Click **Edit the new document now** to create a document and open it in Word.

7. In the **Insert Hyperlink** dialog box, click **OK**.

➤ **To create a hyperlink to a webpage**

1. Select the text or graphic from which you want to link.

2. On the **Insert** tab, in the **Links** group, click the **Hyperlink** button.

3. In the **Insert Hyperlink** dialog box, in the **Link to** list, click **Existing File or Web Page**.

4. In the **Address** box, enter the URL of the webpage you want to link to.

   Or

   Click the **Browse the Web** button. In the web browser window that opens, display the webpage you want to link to. Then minimize or close the browser window.

5. In the **Insert Hyperlink** dialog box, click **OK**.

➤ **To create a hyperlink to a heading or bookmark within the message**

1. Select the text or graphic from which you want to link.

2. On the **Insert** tab, in the **Links** group, click the **Hyperlink** button.

3. In the **Insert Hyperlink** dialog box, in the **Link to** list, click **Place in This Document**.

4. In the **Select a place in this document** box, click the heading or bookmark you want to link to.

5. In the **Insert Hyperlink** dialog box, click **OK**.

➤ **To create a hyperlink that creates a pre-addressed email message**

1. Select the text or graphic from which you want to link.

2. On the **Insert** tab, in the **Links** group, click the **Hyperlink** button.

3. In the **Insert Hyperlink** dialog box, in the **Link to** list, click **E-mail Address**.

4. In the **E-mail address** box, enter the name or email address of the message recipient.

5. In the **Subject** box, enter the message subject.

6. In the **Insert Hyperlink** dialog box, click **OK**.

➤ **To change the target of an existing hyperlink**

1. Right-click the hyperlinked text or graphic, and then click **Edit Hyperlink**.

2. In the **Edit Hyperlink** dialog box, change the properties of the hyperlink, and then click **OK**.

➤ **To remove a hyperlink**

→ Right-click the hyperlinked text or graphic, and then click **Remove Hyperlink**.

Insert images

Email is a means of communicating information to other people, and, as the old saying goes, a picture is worth a thousand words. Using Outlook 2013, you can communicate visual information in the following ways:

- Share photographs with other people by attaching the photos to messages or embedding them in messages.

- Share information from websites, documents, and other visual presentations by capturing images of your screen directly from Outlook and then inserting those images in your message.

- Explain complicated processes and other business information by creating SmartArt graphics within messages or by embedding SmartArt graphics that you create in other Office 2013 programs.

- Communicate statistical information by creating a chart within a message.

- Decorate message content by inserting clip art images.

You can insert all these types of images from the Illustrations group on the Insert tab into the content pane of an email message, calendar item, or task, or into the notes pane of a contact record.

> **Strategy** Capturing screen shots, inserting SmartArt graphics or charts, and formatting images are beyond the scope of this exam.

You can insert digital photographs or pictures created in almost any program into an Outlook email message. You specify the source of the picture you want to insert by clicking one of the following two buttons, which are located in the Illustrations group on the Insert tab:

- **Pictures** Click this button to insert a picture that is saved as a file on your computer, on a network drive, or on a device (such as a digital camera) that is connected to your computer.

- **Online Pictures** Click this button to insert a royalty-free clip art image from Office.com, a web search result from Bing, or an image stored in your personal online storage folder or another online source.

After inserting a picture from a file or from an online source, you can modify the picture and control the flow of text around it by using the commands on the Format tool tab that appears when the picture is selected.

After inserting a picture from a file or online source, you can modify the picture and control the flow of text around it by using the commands on the Format tool tab that appears when the picture is selected.

➤ **To insert an image from a file**

1. In the **Illustrations** group on the **Insert** tab, click the **Pictures** button.

2. In the **Insert Picture** dialog box, browse to and click the file you want. Then do one of the following:

   o Click **Insert** to insert the image on the slide.

   o In the **Insert** list, click **Link to File** to insert an image that updates automatically if the image file changes, or click **Insert and Link** to insert an image that you can manually update if the image file changes.

➤ **To insert an online image**

1. In the **Illustrations** group on the **Insert** tab, click the **Online Pictures** button.

2. In the **Insert Pictures** window, click the online source.

3. Enter a keyword in the search box and press **Enter**, or browse to the picture you want to insert.

4. Double-click the image you want to insert.

> **Tip** You change the size, shape, and location of an image by using the same techniques as you do with other graphic elements.

Insert memorized content

You can save information and document elements that you use frequently as custom building blocks so that you can easily insert them into documents. A custom building block can be a simple phrase or sentence that you use often, or it can include full paragraphs of text and objects such as graphics. You need to create the element exactly as you want it only one time; then you can save it as a building block and use it confidently wherever you need it. You insert a custom building block into a document from the Quick Parts gallery on the Quick Parts menu.

To create a building block, you create and select the item you want to save, click Save Selection To Quick Parts Gallery on the Quick Parts menu, and assign a name to the building block. You can then insert the building block at the cursor by entering the building block name and pressing F3, or by displaying the Quick Parts gallery and clicking the thumbnail of the building block you want. Or you can insert it elsewhere by right-clicking the thumbnail in the gallery and then clicking one of the specified locations.

➤ **To create Quick Parts**

1. In a message composition window, enter and format the content you want to save as a Quick Part.

2. Select the content.

3. On the **Insert** tab, in the **Text** group, click the **Quick Parts** button, and then click **Save Selection to Quick Part Gallery**.

4. In the **Create New Building Block** dialog box, do the following, and then click **OK**:

    a. In the **Name** box, enter a name for the building block.

    b. In the **Description** box, enter a description that will appear as a ScreenTip when you point to the building block in the Quick Parts gallery.

➤ **To insert Quick Parts**

→ Enter the building block name, and then press **F3**.

→ On the **Insert** tab, in the **Text** group, click the **Quick Parts** button, and then click the building block you want to insert.

Insert signatures

After you create a signature, you can manually add it to any email message. Inserting a signature in a message automatically replaces any signature that is already in the message.

> **See Also** For information about creating and assigning email signatures, see section 1.1, "Customize Outlook settings."

➤ **To manually insert an existing email signature in a message**

1. Position the cursor where you want to insert the email signature.

2. On the **Insert** tab, in the **Include** group, click the **Signature** button.

3. In the **Signature** list, click the name of the email signature you want to insert.

➤ **To remove an email signature from a message**

→ Select and delete the signature content as you would any other text.

Practice tasks

The practice file for these tasks is located in the MOSOutlook2013\Objective2 practice file folder. Save the results of the tasks in the same folder.

- Create a message with the subject *MOS Formatting*. Open the *Outlook_2-2* document. Select all the content in the document and copy it to the Microsoft Office Clipboard. Paste the copied content into the *MOS Formatting* message as unformatted text.

- In the *MOS Formatting* message, format the pasted content as follows:
  - Apply the Title style to the first paragraph.
  - Apply the Subtitle style to the second paragraph.
  - Format the four paragraphs representing categories of rules as a bulleted list.
  - Apply the Heading 1 style to the Definitions and General Rules paragraphs.

- Send the *MOS Formatting* message to yourself.

- Create an email message with the subject *MOS Links*. In the message body, enter the following text:

  You can find more information about Microsoft Office 2013 here. Please let me know if you have any questions.

  Insert the following hyperlinks in the message text:
  - A link from the word *here* that displays the Office website at office.microsoft.com in a new window.
  - A link from the words *let me know* that creates an email message addressed to you with the subject *Office help request*.

- Send the *MOS Links* message to yourself.

2.3 Organize and manage messages

Categorize messages

To help you locate Outlook items associated with a specific subject, project, person, or other attribute, you can create a category specific to that attribute and assign the category to any related items. You can assign a category to any type of Outlook item, such as a message, an appointment, a contact record, or a note. For example, you might assign contact records for customers to a Customers category, or contact records, messages, and meetings associated with a specific project to a category named for the project.

Outlook uses color categories, which combine named categories with color bars to provide an immediate visual cue when you view messages in your Inbox, appointments on your calendar, and other information. Depending on the view of the Outlook items, the category might be indicated by a simple colored block or a large colored bar.

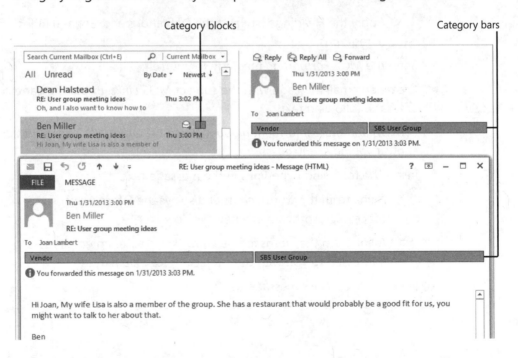

> **Tip** You can locate, sort, and filter Outlook items by category. For information, see section 1.4 "Search in Outlook."

Outlook 2013 has six preconfigured color categories named only by color. You can re-name them and create new categories. Each category can have the following elements:

- **Name** The category name can be one simple word or a long, descriptive phrase. The first 32 characters of the category name are visible in the color categories dia-log box, but pointing to a truncated name displays the entire name in a ScreenTip.

- **Shortcut key** You can assign any of the 11 available keyboard shortcut combina-tions (Ctrl+F2 through Ctrl+F12) to the individual color categories. (You can assign only these 11 keyboard shortcuts within the dialog box.)

- **Color** You can assign any of the 25 available colors to a category (or to multiple categories), or you can choose not to assign a color and to rely only on the name to distinguish between categories. (You can't choose colors other than the 25 shown.) When you assign a category that doesn't have an associated color to an Outlook item, the color block or color bar is shown as white.

You can assign an unlimited number of categories to a message, but only the three most recently assigned appear in the message list. The colors representing all the assigned categories appear in the Reading Pane.

> **Tip** If you don't rename a standard color category before assigning it for the first time, Outlook gives you the option of renaming the category the first time you use it.

Outlook users with Exchange, IMAP, or POP accounts can designate one category as the Quick Click category. Outlook assigns the Quick Click category by default when you sim-ply click the Category box or column associated with an item. (Category boxes appear in the message header in Single view and Preview view.) Until you select a Quick Click cat-egory, clicking the blank Category boxes has no effect.

> ➤ **To assign a color category to an item**

  → In any mail or contact folder, on the **Categorize** menu, in the **Tags** group on the **Home** tab, click the category you want.

  → In any calendar, on the **Categorize** menu, in the **Tags** group on the tool tab (such as **Appointment** or **Meeting**) that appears for the selected item, click the category you want.

  → In any message list view, click the empty box in the **Categories** column to assign the **Quick Click** category.

  > **Tip** You must first set the Quick Click category, as described in the following instructions.

  → In any folder, right-click an item or a selection of items, click **Categorize**, and then click the category you want.

> ➤ **To assign a selected item to multiple color categories**

  1. On the **Categorize** menu, click **All Categories**.

  2. In the **Color Categories** dialog box, select the check boxes of the categories you want, and then click **OK**.

> ➤ **To assign a keyboard shortcut to a color category**

  1. On the **Categorize** menu, click **All Categories**.

  2. In the **Color Categories** dialog box, click the category.

  3. In the **Shortcut Key** list, click the key combination you want.

  4. In the **Color Categories** dialog box, click **OK**.

> ➤ **To rename a color category**

  1. On the **Categorize** menu, click **All Categories**.

  2. In the **Color Categories** dialog box, double-click the category you want to rename, or click the category name and then click **Rename**.

  3. With the category name selected for editing, enter the name you want, and then press **Enter**.

  4. Click **OK**.

➤ **To create a custom color category**

1. On the **Categorize** menu, click **All Categories**.

2. In the **Color Categories** dialog box, click **New**.

3. In the **Name** box of the **Add New Category** dialog box, enter a name for the category.

4. Click the **Color** arrow, and then click the color you want to associate with the new category.

5. Click the **Shortcut Key** arrow, and then click the keyboard shortcut you want.

6. Click **OK** twice.

➤ **To set or change the Quick Click color category**

1. On the **Categorize** menu, click **Set Quick Click**.

2. In the **Set Quick Click** dialog box, select the category you want Outlook to use, and then click **OK**.

> **Tip** You can also set the Quick Click category from the Advanced page of the Outlook Options dialog box. For more information, see section 1.1, "Customize Outlook settings."

Flag messages for follow-up

You can assign a reminder flag for your own reference, to remind you to follow up on a message, contact record, or task. The flags available for messages and tasks are Call, Do Not Forward, Follow Up, For Your Information, Forward, No Response Necessary, Read, Reply, Reply To All, and Review. The flags available for contact records are Follow Up, Call, Arrange Meeting, Send E-mail, and Send Letter. The default flag for any item is Follow Up. Assigning a flag to an email message or contact record adds it to your task list.

If you add a reminder to a flagged item, Outlook displays the Reminders window at the specified time. From the Reminders window, you can dismiss the flag or postpone the reminder to a later time.

You can assign a flag to an outgoing message. If you assign a standard flag, it appears only to you. If you specifically flag the message for recipients, Outlook reminds you and/or the recipient to follow up on the message with a specific action.

➤ **To flag an item for your follow-up**

→ Select the item. On the **Home** tab, in the **Tags** group, click the **Follow Up** button, and then click the flag corresponding to the follow-up time you want to specify.

→ In the content pane, right-click the item, point to **Follow Up**, and then click the flag corresponding to the follow-up time you want to specify.

➤ **To set a custom flag**

1. Select the item. On the **Home** tab, in the **Tags** group, click the **Follow Up** button, and then click **Custom**.

2. In the **Custom** dialog box, in the **Flag to** list, click the flag you want to appear in the item header.

3. Set the start date and due date to control where the item appears on your task list, and then click **OK**.

➤ **To add a reminder to a flagged item**

→ In the **Custom** dialog box, select the **Reminder** check box, and then specify the date and time at which you want the reminder to appear.

   Or

1. On the **Home** tab, in the **Tags** group, click the **Follow Up** button, and then click **Add Reminder**.

2. With the **Reminder** check box selected, specify the reminder date and time, and then click **OK**.

➤ **To flag an outgoing message for your follow-up**

→ On the **Message** tab of the message composition window, in the **Tags** group, click the **Follow Up** button, and then click the flag corresponding to the follow-up time you want to specify.

➤ **To flag an outgoing message for the recipient's follow-up**

1. On the **Message** tab, in the **Tags** group, click the **Follow Up** button, and then click **Custom**.

2. In the **Custom** dialog box, select the **Flag for Recipients** check box.

3. Specify the **Flag to** action and the reminder date and time, and then click **OK**.

Manage conversations

Conversation view is an alternative arrangement of messages grouped by subject. All the messages with the same subject appear together in your Inbox (or other message folder) under one conversation header. You can display differing levels of messages within a conversation. Until you expand the conversation, all the messages grouped within it take up only as much space in your Inbox as a single message would.

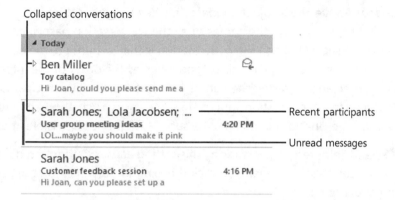

Collapsed conversations

The conversation header provides information about the messages within the conversation, including the number of unread messages and whether one or more messages includes an attachment, is categorized, or is flagged for follow up.

When you receive a message that is part of a conversation, the entire conversation moves to the top of your Inbox and the new message appears when you click the conversation header. When a conversation includes unread messages, a blue vertical line appears to the left of the header and the conversation subject is in bold blue font, just as an unread message would appear. When you have multiple unread messages, the number is indicated in parentheses following the subject. The senders of the unread messages are listed below the subject.

As with other features of Outlook 2013, you can modify the way Conversation view displays messages to suit the way you work.

Conversation view settings include:

- **Show Messages from Other Folders** By default, Conversation view displays messages stored in any folder, including sent messages that are stored in the Sent Items folder. (Within the expanded conversation, sent messages are indicated by italic font.) You can turn off this setting to display only messages from the current folder.

- **Show Senders Above the Subject** By default, when a conversation is collapsed, the conversation header displays the names of all the conversation participants above the conversation subject; when the conversation is fully expanded, the conversation header displays only the subject. This setting reverses the order of the information in the conversation header; the names of the conversation participants are displayed above the conversation subject. In some cases, such as when Outlook displays a message on the second line, the subject might not be visible at all.

- **Always Expand Selected Conversation** This setting causes Outlook to display all messages in a conversation when you click the Expand Conversation button or conversation header once.

- **Use Classic Indented View** This setting causes Outlook to indent older messages within individual message threads to show the progression of the thread. This setting is not as effective as the default for displaying split conversations because a message might be at the root of multiple branches but can appear only once in the message list.

With Conversation view, you can manage all the messages within a conversation as a group. You can do this by clicking the conversation header to effectively select all the messages in the conversation (they won't appear selected, but, for example, moving the conversation header to another folder moves all the individual messages in the conversation) and then applying your action. Or you can use these very useful conversation-management tools:

- **Ignore Conversation** This command moves the selected conversation and any related messages you receive in the future directly to the Deleted Items folder.

- **Clean Up Conversation** This command deletes redundant messages—messages whose text is wholly contained within later messages—from a conversation. By default, Outlook doesn't clean up categorized, flagged, or digitally signed messages. You can modify conversation clean-up settings on the Mail page of the Outlook Options dialog box.

➤ **To turn Conversation view on or off**

→ On the **View** tab, in the **Messages** group, select or clear the **Show as Conversations** check box.

➤ **To select one or more Conversation view options**

→ In the **Messages** group, click the **Conversation Settings** button, and then click **Show Messages from Other Folders**, **Show Senders Above the Subject**, **Always Expand Selected Conversation**, or **Use Classic Indented View**.

➤ **To expand a conversation**

→ Click the conversation header or the **Expand Conversation** button to the left of the conversation header once to display the most recent message in the **Reading Pane** and to display all the unique messages in the conversation.

→ Click the **Expand Conversation** button twice to display all messages in the conversation, including messages from your **Sent Items** folder.

➤ **To delete redundant messages in a conversation**

1. Select one or more messages or conversations.

2. On the **Home** tab, in the **Delete** group, click the **Clean Up** button.

3. In the **Clean Up** list, do one of the following:

   ○ To delete all redundant messages from the selected conversations, click **Clean Up Conversation** and then, in the **Clean Up Conversation** dialog box, click **Clean Up**.

   ○ To delete all redundant messages from the current folder but not its sub-folders, click **Clean Up Folder** and then, in the **Clean Up Folder** dialog box, click **Clean Up Folder**.

   ○ To delete all redundant messages from the current folder and its subfolders, click **Clean Up Folder & Subfolders** and then, in the **Clean Up Folder** dialog box, click **Clean Up Folder**.

➤ **To delete all current and future messages in a conversation**

→ Press **Ctrl+Del** to ignore the currently active conversation.

   Or

1. Select one or more messages or conversations.

2. On the **Home** tab, in the **Delete** group, click the **Ignore** button.

3. In the **Ignore Conversation** dialog box, click **Ignore Conversation**.

Organize messages in folders

You can create folders to contain email messages, calendar information, contact records, and other items. You must specify the type of items the folder will contain when you create it.

➤ **To create folders**

1. On the **Folder** tab, in the **New** group, click the **New Folder** button.

2. In the **Create New Folder** dialog box, enter a name for the folder in the **Name** box, and then in the **Folder contains** list, click **Calendar Items**, **Contact Items**, **InfoPath Form Items**, **Journal Items**, **Mail and Post Items**, **Note Items**, or **Task Items**.

3. In the **Select where to place the folder** list, click the location in which you want to create the folder.

4. In the **Create New Folder** dialog box, click **OK**.

➤ **To move selected messages between folders**

→ Drag the messages to the folder in the **Folder Pane**.

→ On the **Home** tab, in the **Move** group, click **Move**, and then click the folder to which you want to move the messages.

   Or

1. On the **Home** tab, in the **Move** group, click **Move**, and then click **Other Folder**.

2. In the **Move Items** dialog box, click the folder to which you want to move the messages, and then click **OK**.

Manage junk email

By default, when Outlook receives a message that it deems to be either junk mail or a phishing message, it delivers that message to the Junk E-mail folder associated with your account rather than to your Inbox. (Each account you configure Outlook to connect to has its own Junk E-mail folder.) When the Junk E-mail folder contains one or more messages, the number of messages in the folder is shown in parentheses at the end of the folder name. If any of the messages in the folder have not been read, the folder name is bold.

Outlook converts message content in the Junk E-mail folder to plain text and disables any active links or content within the message. The InfoBar in the message header provides specific information about the message's status.

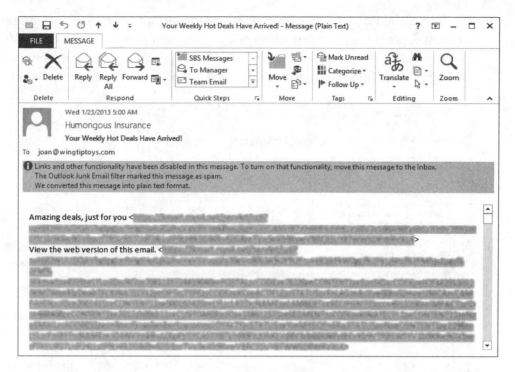

Any remote graphics (graphics that are displayed from Internet locations rather than embedded in the message—sometimes called *web beacons*) that were present in the message are converted to URLs, which reveals where the graphics originated.

Although the response options on the ribbon are active, you can't reply to a message from the Junk E-mail folder—you must first move it to the Inbox or another folder. You can delete messages from the Junk E-mail folder, or forward a message from the folder to someone else who can verify for you whether the message is valid. The forwarded message will be in plain-text format rather than in the original message format.

You manage junk mail settings from the Junk E-mail Options dialog box. You set specific junk email processing options for each email account to which Outlook is configured to connect. The account for which you're configuring options is shown in the title bar of the Junk E-mail Options dialog box. The Junk E-mail Options dialog box has five pages.

➤ **To process a junk mail message**

1. In the **Junk E-mail** folder, select the message you want to process.

2. On the **Home** tab, in the **Delete** group, click the **Junk** button.

3. In the **Junk** list, click one of the following:

- **Block Sender** to add the message sender to the Blocked Senders list.

- **Never Block Sender** to add the message sender to the Safe Senders list.

- **Never Block Sender's Domain** to add the message sender's domain to the Safe Senders list.

- **Never Block this Group or Mailing List** to add the group to which the message was sent to the Safe Recipients list.

- **Not Junk** to move the message to the Inbox. You then have the option of adding the message sender to the Safe Senders list.

➤ **To configure junk mail settings for the sender of an open message**

➜ On the **Message** tab of the message reading window, in the **Delete** group, click the **Junk** button, and then click the option you want.

➤ **To empty the Junk E-mail folder of any mailbox**

1. Display the **Folder List** in the **Folder Pane** and expand the mailbox to display its **Junk E-mail** folder.

2. Right-click the **Junk E-mail** folder, and then click **Empty Folder**.

3. In the message box that appears, click **Yes** to confirm that you want to permanently delete the items.

➤ **To open the Junk E-mail Options dialog box**

→ On the **Home** tab, in the **Delete** group, on the **Junk** menu, click **Junk E-mail Options**.

➤ **To choose a junk email protection level**

→ On the **Options** page of the **Junk E-mail Options** dialog box, click **No Automatic Filtering**, **Low**, **High**, or **Safe Lists Only**.

➤ **To configure Outlook to automatically delete suspected junk email**

→ On the **Options** page of the **Junk E-mail Options** dialog box, select the **Permanently delete suspected junk e-mail instead of moving it to the Junk E-mail folder** check box.

Tip Do not select the Permanently Delete Suspected Junk E-Mail... check box if you set the protection level to High or to Safe Lists Only. With these settings, it is likely that the Junk E-Mail Filter will catch quite a few valid messages that you don't want deleted.

➤ **To ensure that messages from a specific sender or domain aren't classified as junk**

1. On the **Safe Senders** page of the **Junk E-mail Options** dialog box, click **Add**.

2. In the **Add address or domain** dialog box, enter an email address (for example, *tom@contoso.com*) or domain (for example, *@contoso.com*), and then click **OK**.

➤ **To ensure that responses to messages you send aren't classified as junk**

→ On the **Safe Senders** page of the **Junk E-mail Options** dialog box, select the **Automatically add people I e-mail to the Safe Senders List** check box.

➤ **To ensure that messages sent to a specific email address or domain aren't classified as junk**

1. On the **Safe Recipients** page of the **Junk E-mail Options** dialog box, click **Add**.

2. In the **Add address or domain** dialog box, enter an email address or domain, and then click **OK**.

Tip Add distribution lists or mailing lists of which you are a member to your Safe Recipients List to ensure that messages sent to you through the distribution list or mailing list will never be treated as junk email.

➤ **To ensure that messages from a specific sender or domain are always classified as junk**

1. On the **Blocked Senders** page of the **Junk E-mail Options** dialog box, click **Add**.

2. In the **Add address or domain** dialog box, enter an email address or domain, and then click **OK**.

➤ **To block all messages from a location-specific top-level domain**

1. On the **International** page of the **Junk E-mail Options** dialog box, click the **Blocked Top-Level Domain List** button.

2. In the **Blocked Top-Level Domain List** dialog box, select the check box for each country or region you want to block, and then click **OK**.

➤ **To block all messages with language-specific encoding**

1. On the **International** page of the **Junk E-mail Options** dialog box, click the **Blocked Encodings List** button.

2. In the **Blocked Encodings List** dialog box, select the check box for each language you want to block, and then click **OK**.

Practice tasks

There are no practice files for these tasks.

- Create a subfolder of your Inbox named *Important*.
- In your Inbox, assign two messages to the blue category and two messages to the green category.
- Create a new color category named *Management* that uses the orange color, and the Ctrl+F2 keyboard shortcut. Then assign one blue message and one green message to the Management category.
- Filter your mailbox to display all items assigned to the Management category, and move the items to the Important folder.
- Display the contents of your Inbox in Conversation view. Identify a conversation with multiple threads, and delete the redundant messages in the conversation by using the Clean Up command.
- In your Inbox, use a message from someone you trust to add that person's email address to your Safe Senders list.
- Locate a junk mail message in your Inbox, Junk Mail folder, or other folder. Add the message sender to your Blocked Senders list.
- If your Junk E-mail folder contains no messages you want to keep, empty it.

Objective review

Before finishing this chapter, ensure that you have mastered the following skills:

2.1 Create messages

2.2 Format messages

2.3 Organize and manage messages

3 Manage schedules

The skills tested in this section of the Microsoft Office Specialist exam for Microsoft Outlook 2013 relate to managing calendars, calendar items, tasks, notes, and journal entries. Specifically, the following objectives are associated with this set of skills:

3.1 Create and manage calendars

3.2 Create appointments, meetings, and events

3.3 Organize and manage appointments, meetings, and events

3.4 Create and manage notes, tasks, and journals

Using the Microsoft Outlook 2013 calendar is a big step toward efficient time management. You can track appointments and events, and organize meetings. The Outlook calendar differentiates between working time and nonworking time—only working time is available to co-workers when they schedule meetings with you through Outlook. You can also configure the Outlook calendar to track your schedule in two time zones and smoothly switch between time zones when you travel.

In addition to the default Outlook calendar, you can create, import, link to, subscribe to, and manage other calendars within the Calendar module. And you can share your calendar information with other people in several ways; for example, you can share an entire calendar or only selected information with people inside or outside of your organization.

Outlook provides other modules in which to track information. The Tasks module provides a way to track independent tasks and messages that you want to follow up on, and to assign tasks to other people. You can display your daily task lists in the calendar to coordinate the time required to complete them. You can save general information in the Notes module. And you can record interactions that you have with specific people in the Outlook Journal module.

This chapter guides you in studying ways of managing calendars, appointments, meetings, and events; tracking tasks; and recording information in notes and journal entries.

> **Practice Files** To complete the practice tasks in this chapter, you need the practice file contained in the MOSOutlook2013\Objective3 practice file folder. For more information, see "Download the practice files" in this book's Introduction.

3.1 Create and manage calendars

Configure calendar settings

The Calendar module offers four distinct views of content. These views are:

- **Calendar** This is the standard view in which you display your Outlook calendar. In the Day, Work Week, or Week arrangement, Calendar view displays the subject, location, and organizer (if space allows) of each appointment, meeting, or event, in addition to the availability bar and any special icons, such as Private or Recurrence.

- **Preview** In the Day, Work Week, or Week arrangement, this view displays additional information, including information from the notes area of the appointment window, as space allows.

- **List** This list view displays all appointments, meetings, and events on your calendar.

- **Active** This list view displays only future appointments, meetings, and events.

In your Outlook calendar, the time that you indicate you are available for other people to schedule meetings with you is referred to as your *work week*. The calendar time slots within your work week are colored differently from those outside of your work week, and are the only time slots made available to people on your network when they are searching for a time to meet with you.

Working time   Nonworking time

By default, the Outlook work week is defined as from 8:00 A.M. to 5:00 P.M. (in your local time zone), Monday through Friday. You can change this to match your individual work schedule. In Outlook 2013, you can specify a start time and end time for your standard work day, specify the days of the week that you work, and specify the day of the week that you'd like to appear first when you display only the work week in your calendar.

> **Tip** Outlook doesn't allow you to define a workday that crosses midnight or to define different start and end times for different days.

If you frequently travel or work with colleagues or clients outside of your usual time zone, you might want to change the time zone on your computer so that information such as the receipt time of email messages, appointment times, and the time on the clock in the Windows Taskbar notification area reflects your current location. If you have appointments in both time zones, you can display both time zones on the left side of the Calendar pane, and swap between zones when you travel. That way, you can be sure to correctly enter appointments at the time they will occur in their respective time zones.

➤ **To display a different calendar view**

→ On the **View** tab, in the **Current View** group, click the **Change View** button, and then click **Calendar**, **Preview**, **List**, or **Active**.

➤ **To modify the time period shown in Calendar view or Preview view**

→ On the **View** tab, in the **Arrangement** group, click the **Day**, **Work Week**, **Week**, or **Month** button.

→ In the **Arrangement** group, click the **Schedule View** button. Then in the **Time Scale** list, click **60 Minutes**, **30 Minutes**, **15 Minutes**, **10 Minutes**, **6 Minutes**, or **5 Minutes**.

➤ **To modify the grouping of calendar items in List view or Active view**

→ On the **View** tab, in the **Arrangement** gallery, click **Categories**, **Start Date**, **Recurrence**, or **Location**.

→ Right-click any column heading, and then click **Group By This Field**.

➤ **To sort calendar items in List view or Active view**

→ Click any column heading to sort by the values in that column.

→ Click the active sort column heading to reverse the sort order.

→ On the **View** tab, in the **Arrangement** group, click the **Reverse Sort** button.

➤ **To set work times on the default calendar**

1. Open the **Outlook Options** dialog box. On the **Calendar** page, in the **Work time** area, set the start time and end time of the work day you want to define.

2. In the **Work week** area, select the check boxes of the days you want to include in your work week.

3. In the **First day of week** list, click the day you want to appear first (on the left) in the **Work Week** view of your calendar.

4. In the **First week of year** list, click **Starts on Jan 1**, **First 4-day week**, or **First full week**.

➤ **To change the calendar time zone**

1. Open the **Outlook Options** dialog box. On the **Calendar** page, in the **Time zones** area, click the **Time zone** list, and then click the time zone you want to display.

2. In the corresponding **Label** box, enter a description of up to 32 characters.

➤ **To display multiple time zones**

1. On the **Calendar** page of the **Outlook Options** dialog box, in the **Time zones** area, select the **Show a second time zone** check box.

2. In the corresponding **Time zone** list, click the second time zone you want to display.

3. In the corresponding **Label** box, enter a description of up to 32 characters.

➤ **To switch your calendar between the primary and secondary time zones**

→ On the **Calendar** page of the **Outlook Options** dialog box, in the **Time zones** area, click the **Swap Time Zones** button.

Work with multiple calendars

The Calendar button on the Navigation Bar links to the calendar of your default email account. In addition, you can display the following types of calendars in the Calendar module:

- **Calendars of your other email accounts** These are available automatically when you configure Outlook to connect to an account.

- **Custom calendars** You create a calendar in the same way that you do a folder that contains mail, contact records, or other items.

- **Calendars of people within your organization** Within an organization that uses Microsoft Exchange Server, you can display the availability of your co-workers, individually or in a group, without special permission.

- **Shared calendars** Other Outlook users can share their calendars with you.

- **SharePoint site calendars** You can connect a SharePoint calendar to Outlook.

- **Internet calendars** You can subscribe to or import calendars from the Internet.

All these types of calendars are available to you from the Folder Pane in the Calendar module or the Folder List in the Mail module.

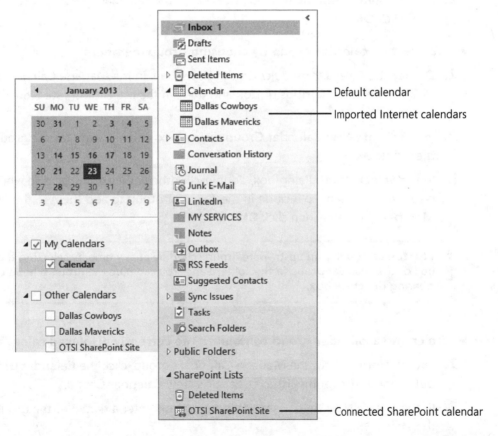

You can display calendars individually, or you can display more than one calendar at a time. For example, you might have separate business and personal calendars and want to view them together. You can view multiple calendars next to each other, or you can overlay them to display a composite view of the separate calendars. When you view and scroll through multiple calendars, they all display the same date or time period.

➤ **To display or hide multiple calendars**

→ In the **Folder Pane** of the Calendar module, select or clear the check box of individual calendars.

→ In the **Folder Pane** of the Mail module, expand the **Folder List**, and then click a calendar to display it.

➤ **To create a secondary calendar**

1. Display the Calendar module. On the **Folder** tab, in the **New** group, click the **New Calendar** button.

2. In the **Create New Folder** dialog box, name the calendar, select its location, and then click **OK**.

➤ **To create a calendar group by choosing group members**

1. Display the Calendar module. On the **Home** tab, in the **Manage Calendars** group, click the **Calendar Groups** button and then, in the list, click **Create New Calendar Group**.

2. In the **Create New Calendar Group** dialog box, enter a name for the group, and then click **OK**.

3. In the **Select Name** dialog box, double-click the names of the people whose calendars you want to include in the calendar group to add them to the **Group Members** box, and then click **OK**.

> **Tip** You can display an up-to-date group schedule at any time by selecting the check box of the calendar group in the Folder Pane. You can hide the group schedule by clearing the check box.

➤ **To create a calendar group containing the currently displayed calendars**

1. On the **Home** tab, in the **Manage Calendars** group, click the **Calendar Groups** button and then, in the list, click **Save as New Calendar Group**.

2. In the **Create New Calendar Group** dialog box, enter a name for the group, and then click **OK**.

➤ **To delete a calendar group**

1. In the **Folder Pane**, right-click the name of the calendar group, and then click **Delete Group**.

2. In the confirmation dialog box, click **Yes**.

➤ **To delete a calendar from the Calendar module or from a calendar group**

→ In the **Folder Pane**, right-click the calendar name, and then click **Delete Calendar**.

➤ **To switch between Overlay Mode and Side-By-Side Mode**

→ On the title bar tab of any secondary calendar, click the **View in Overlay Mode** button. In Overlay Mode, click either calendar tab to display that calendar on top of the other calendar.

→ On any overlaid calendar, click the **View in Side-By-Side Mode** button to return to the standard display.

→ Right-click any calendar tab, and then click **Overlay** to turn Overlay Mode on or off for that calendar.

Share calendar information

Co-workers can view your available working time when they schedule meetings with you or view your calendar through Outlook. If you want to share more information with co-workers or with people outside of your organization, you have several options for doing so.

- You can allow selected co-workers to view calendar item details by sharing the calendar with them.

- You can allow selected co-workers to view your entire calendar and to make appointments and respond to meeting requests on your behalf by delegating control of the calendar to them.

- You can publish your calendar to the Office.com website or to a corporate web server and then share the published calendar with any person who has access to the Internet.

- You can send a professional graphic representation of your appointments during a selected date range by email to any person who uses an HTML-capable email program (not only people who use Outlook), including colleagues, friends, and family members.

The options for sending, sharing, and publishing calendar information are available from the Share group on the Home tab of the Calendar module.

> **See Also** For information about delegating access to your calendar, see "Delegate access" in section 2.1, "Create messages."

If your email address is part of an Exchange network, you can give permission to other people on your network to view, modify, or create items within a calendar or any other type of Outlook folder. The level of access each co-worker has is governed by the permissions you assign to him or her. Using this method, you can share your default calendar or a secondary calendar that you create, import, or subscribe to.

After you share a calendar, you can specify the actions each person with whom you share the calendar can take. You can select a permission level, which includes Read, Write, Delete, and other settings, or you can select individual settings in each category.

> **Tip** From the Permissions page, you can change the default permission level to your calendar and permit co-workers to view more information than only your availability.

➤ **To share a calendar**

1. In the Calendar module, display the calendar you want to share.

2. On the **Home** tab, in the **Share** group, click the **Share Calendar** button to create a sharing invitation.

3. Address the invitation to the person with whom you'd like to share your calendar. If you'd like to request that the person reciprocate by sharing his or her calendar with you, select the **Request permission to view recipient's Calendar** check box.

4. In the **Details** list, click the level of detail you want to share: **Availability only**, **Limited details**, or **Full details**.

5. Add any notes you want to in the content pane, send the message, and then click **Yes** in the **Microsoft Outlook** dialog box that asks you to confirm that you want to share the calendar with the specified permissions.

➤ **To configure permissions for a shared calendar**

1. On the **Home** tab, in the **Share** group, click the **Calendar Permissions** button.

2. On the **Permissions** page of the **Calendar Properties** dialog box, click a pre-configured permission level in the **Permission Level** list, or select individual options.

Practice tasks

There are no practice files for these tasks. Before you begin, alert a colleague that you are going to practice sharing your calendar.

- Display your primary calendar for next month.

- Display only the second week of the month.

- Display only the fifteenth day of the month.

- Create a secondary calendar named *MOS Schedule*, and display it beside your primary calendar.

- Create a calendar group named *MOS Team* that includes the secondary calendar and the calendar of a colleague, and display the calendar group in Schedule view.

- Display the MOS Team calendar group in Overlay Mode.

- Delete the MOS Team calendar group.

- Hide the MOS Schedule calendar.

3.2 Create appointments, meetings, and events

Create appointments and events

Appointments are blocks of time you schedule for only yourself (as opposed to meetings, to which you invite other people). An appointment has a specific start time and end time.

Events occur for one or more 24-hour days—for example, a birthday, a vacation week, or anything else occurring on specific days but not beginning and ending at specific times. In all other respects, creating an event is identical to creating an appointment, in that you can specify a location, indicate recurrence, indicate your availability, and attach additional information to the event item.

You can schedule a simple appointment or event directly on the calendar, or provide additional details in an appointment window. The minimum requirements are a subject and a time slot. You can also include the appointment location and enter additional information (including formatted text, website links, and even file attachments) in a notes area so that it is readily available to you at the time of the appointment.

When creating an appointment, meeting, or event, you indicate your availability (also referred to as *Free/Busy time*) by marking it as Free, Working Elsewhere, Tentative, Busy, or Out Of Office. The appointment time is color-coded on your calendar to match the availability you indicate. Your availability is visible to other Outlook users on your network, and is also displayed when you share your calendar or send calendar information to other people.

> **To create an appointment with the default settings**

1. In the Calendar module, display the date on which you want to schedule the appointment.

2. In the **Calendar** pane, click the desired time slot, or drag through consecutive time slots.

3. Enter the information you want to appear as the appointment subject, and then press **Enter**.

> **To open a new appointment window**

→ In the Calendar module, on the **Home** tab, in the **New** group, click the **New Appointment** button.

→ In the Calendar module, press **Ctrl+N**.

→ In any module, on the **Home** tab, in the **New** group, click the **New Items** button, and then click **Appointment**.

→ In any module, press **Ctrl+Shift+A**.

> **To create an appointment with custom settings**

1. Open a new appointment window.

2. In the appointment window, enter the information you want to appear on the calendar in the **Subject** and **Location** boxes.

3. Click or enter the appointment start date in the left **Start time** list and, if the appointment extends across multiple days, click or enter the appointment end date in the left **End time** list.

4. Click or enter the appointment start time in the right **Start time** list and the appointment end time in the right **End time** list.

5. On the **Appointment** tab, in the **Options** group, click your availability during the specified appointment time—**Free**, **Working Elsewhere**, **Tentative**, **Busy**, or **Out of Office**—in the **Show As** list.

6. In the **Options** group, in the **Reminder** list, click the length of time prior to the appointment (or **None**) when you would like Outlook to display an appointment reminder.

7. On the **Appointment** tab, in the **Actions** group, click the **Save & Close** button.

➤ **To create an appointment from an email message**

1. In the Mail module, drag the message from the **Mail** pane to the **Calendar** button on the **Navigation Bar**.

2. In the appointment window that opens, edit the appointment details as necessary.

3. On the **Appointment** tab, in the **Actions** group, click the **Save & Close** button.

➤ **To create an event with default settings**

1. Display the calendar in **Day** view, **Work Week** view, or **Week** view, or **Month** view.

2. In the **Calendar** pane, click the space that contains the date (in views other than Month view, the space below the day header and above the time slots).

3. Enter the event name, and then press **Enter**.

➤ **To create an event with custom settings**

➜ In an appointment window header, to the right of the **Start time** boxes, select the **All day event** check box.

Create meetings

A primary difficulty when scheduling a meeting is finding a time that works for all the people who need to attend it. Scheduling meetings through Outlook is significantly simpler than other methods of scheduling meetings, particularly when you need to accommodate the schedules of several people. Outlook displays the individual and collective schedules of people within your own organization, and of people outside of your organization who have published their calendars to the Internet. You can review attendees' schedules to locate a time when everyone is available, or have Outlook find a convenient time for you.

You can send an Outlook meeting invitation (referred to as a *meeting request*) to any person who has an email account—even to a person who doesn't use Outlook. You can send a meeting request from any type of email account (such as an Exchange account or an Internet email account).

The meeting window has two pages: the Appointment page and the Scheduling Assistant page. The Appointment page is visible by default. You can enter all the required information directly on the Appointment page, or use the additional features available on the Scheduling Assistant page to find the best time for the meeting.

The Room Finder is open by default on the right side of each page of the meeting window. This handy tool helps you to identify dates and times that work for the greatest number of attendees, in addition to available locations. The monthly calendar at the top of the Room Finder indicates the collective availability of the group on each day, as follows:

- Dates that occur in the past and nonworking days are gray.

- Days when all attendees are available are white (Good).

- Days when most attendees are available are light blue (Fair).

- Days when most attendees are not available are medium blue (Poor).

> **Tip** All the capabilities for the Room Finder are available for Exchange accounts, but functionality is limited for other types of accounts. You can display or hide the Room Finder page by clicking the Room Finder button in the Options group on the Meeting tab.

Managed conference rooms that are available at the indicated meeting time are shown in the center of the Room Finder. At the bottom of the Room Finder, the Suggested

Times list displays attendee availability for appointments of the length of time you have specified for the meeting.

People you invite to meetings are referred to as *attendees*. By default, the attendance of each attendee is indicated as Required. You can inform noncritical attendees of the meeting by marking their attendance as Optional. You can invite entire groups of people by using a contact group or distribution list. You can also invite managed resources, such as conference rooms and audio/visual equipment, that have been set up by your organization's Exchange administrator.

A meeting request should have at least one attendee other than you, and must have a start time and an end time. It should also include a subject and a location, but Outlook will send the meeting request without this information if you specifically allow it. The body of a meeting request can include text and web links, and you can also attach files. This is a convenient way to distribute meeting information to attendees ahead of time.

The secondary page of the meeting window is the Scheduling Assistant page, if your email account is part of an Exchange Server network. Otherwise, the secondary page is the Scheduling page, which doesn't include the Room Finder feature.

The Scheduling and Scheduling Assistant pages include a group schedule that shows the status of each attendee's time throughout your working day. Outlook indicates your suggested meeting time on the group schedule. If free/busy information is available for meeting attendees, the status is indicated by the standard free/busy colors and patterns that match the legend at the bottom of the page. If no information is available (either because Outlook can't connect to an attendee's calendar or because the proposed meeting is further out than the scheduling information stored on the server), Outlook shows the time with gray diagonal stripes. The row at the top of the schedule, to the right of the All Attendees heading, indicates the collective schedule of all the attendees.

➤ **To open a new meeting window**

→ In the Calendar module, on the **Home** tab, in the **New** group, click the **New Meeting** button.

→ In any module, on the **Home** tab, in the **New** group, click the **New Items** button, and then click **Meeting**.

→ In any module, press **Ctrl+Shift+Q**.

➤ **To create a meeting from an email message**

→ In the message reading window, on the **Message** tab, in the **Respond** group, click the **Meeting** button.

➤ **To convert an appointment or event to a meeting**

→ In an appointment or event window, on the item-specific tab, in the **Attendees** group, click the **Invite Attendees** button.

→ In an appointment or event window, on the item-specific tab, in the **Show** group, click the **Scheduling Assistant** button.

➤ **To invite attendees and schedule resources**

→ On the **Appointment** page of the meeting window, enter the email addresses or names of the attendees or resources in the **To** box.

→ On the **Scheduling** or **Scheduling Assistant** page of the meeting window, enter the email addresses or names of the attendees and resources in the **All Attendees** list.

Or

1. On the **Appointment** page of the meeting window, click the **To** button.

2. In the **Select Attendees and Resources** dialog box, locate and double-click the names of the contacts and managed resources you want to invite, and then click **OK**.

➤ **To invite optional attendees**

1. Invite the attendee by using any of the previously discussed methods.

2. On the **Meeting** tab, in the **Show** group, click the **Scheduling Assistant** button.

3. In the **All Attendees** list, click the icon immediately to the left of the optional attendee's name and then, in the list, click **Optional Attendee**.

➤ **To use the Room Finder**

→ To display suggested meeting times, click a date in the **Date Navigator** at the top of the **Room Finder** pane.

→ To update the meeting request, click a meeting time in the **Suggested Times** list.

Manage calendar items

If you have the same appointment on a regular basis—for example, a bimonthly haircut or a weekly exercise class—you can set it up in your Outlook calendar as a *recurring appointment*. A recurring appointment can happen at almost any regular interval, such as every Tuesday and Thursday, every other week, or the last day of every month. Configuring an appointment recurrence creates multiple instances of the appointment in your calendar at the time interval you specify. You can set the appointment to recur until further notice, to end after a certain number of occurrences, or to end by a certain date. The individual appointments are linked. When making changes to a recurring appointment, you can choose to update all occurrences or only an individual occurrence of the appointment.

➤ **To configure recurrence for calendar items**

1. On the item-specific tab of the item window, in the **Options** group, click the **Recurrence** button.

   Or

   In the **Calendar** pane, select the calendar item. On the item-specific tool tab, in the **Options** group, click the **Recurrence** button.

2. In the **Appointment Recurrence** dialog box, do the following, and then click **OK**:

   a. In the **Recurrence pattern** area, click a frequency option.

   b. In the adjacent area, which changes according to the frequency option you select, adjust the settings to reflect the recurrence you want.

   c. In the **Range of recurrence** area, select the appropriate end date for the series of appointments or events.

➤ **To categorize calendar items**

→ On the item-specific tab of the item window, in the **Tags** group, click the **Categorize** button, and then click the category you want to assign.

→ In the **Calendar** pane, select the calendar item. On the item-specific tool tab, in the **Tags** group, click the **Categorize** button, and then click the category you want to assign.

→ In the **Calendar** pane, right-click the calendar item, click **Categorize**, and then click the category you want to assign.

➤ **To change the time of an existing calendar item**

→ In the **Calendar** pane, drag the item to a different date or to a different time slot.

→ In the **Calendar** pane, in **Day** view, **Work Week** view, or **Week** view, drag the top or bottom border of an appointment or meeting up or down to change the start or end time.

→ In the **Calendar** pane, click an appointment or meeting one time to select it, press **Ctrl+X**, click the time slot to which you want to move the item, and then press **Ctrl+V**.

→ In the item window, adjust the **Start time** and **End time** settings. Then on the item-specific tab, in the **Actions** group, click the **Save & Close** button.

➤ **To create a copy of an existing appointment**

1. In the **Calendar** pane, display the original appointment day and the day to which you want to copy the appointment.

2. Hold down the **Ctrl** key, and drag the appointment to the new date or time slot.

Practice tasks

The practice file for these tasks is located in the MOSOutlook2013\Objective3 practice file folder. Before you begin, alert two colleagues that you are going to practice scheduling meetings.

- Display tomorrow's date in the Calendar pane. Create a half-hour appointment from 11:30 A.M. to 12:00 P.M., with the subject *MOS Lunch with Jane*. Accept all other default settings.

- Without opening the appointment window, change the start time of the MOS Lunch with Jane appointment to 10:30 A.M and the end time to 11:30 A.M.

- Specify the location of the MOS Lunch with Jane appointment as *Fourth Coffee*. Set the appointment options so that other Outlook users know that you will be out of the office from 10:30 A.M. to 11:30 A.M. but can't view any appointment details.

- Create a recurring one-hour appointment on the first Monday of the month at 6:00 P.M. with the subject *MOS Book Club*. Set the series to end after six occurrences.

- Create a two-day event on Tuesday and Wednesday two weeks from now in Portland, Oregon, with the subject *MOS Annual Meeting and Retreat*. Attach the *Outlook_3-2* document to the event.

- Create a request for a half-hour meeting with a colleague, with the subject *MOS Status Meeting*, at 3:00 P.M. tomorrow. Enter *Test – please accept* in the Location box, and send the request to one person.

- Add a second colleague as an optional attendee to the meeting request for the MOS Status Meeting, and then send the meeting request only to the new attendee.

- Schedule a one-hour *MOS Budget Meeting* with two colleagues at the first available time next week. Set up this meeting to occur at the same time every month for three months.

3.3 Organize and manage appointments, meetings, and events

Configure settings for calendar items

As you can with other Outlook items, you can set the importance of a calendar item. Unlike other items, however, the importance is visible only in the open item window. However, you can use the importance setting, as you can any tag, as a way of locating specific calendar items.

By default, Outlook displays a reminder message 15 minutes before the start time of an appointment or meeting, and 18 hours before an all-day event—you can change the reminder to occur as far as two weeks in advance, or you can turn it off completely if you want to.

You might find it necessary to change the date, time, or location of an appointment, meeting, or event. When you are the meeting organizer, you can change any information in a meeting request at any time, including adding or removing invited attendees.

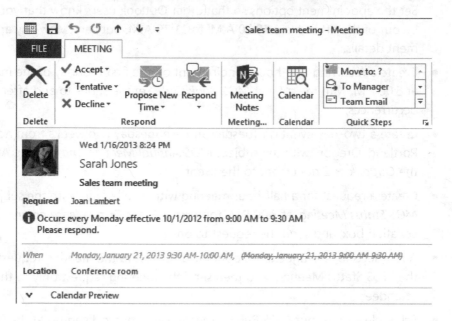

To cancel a meeting, click the meeting on your calendar or open the meeting window, and then click the Cancel Meeting button in the Actions group on the Meeting or Meeting Series tab.

After you edit or cancel a meeting, Outlook sends an updated meeting request to the invited attendees to keep them informed. If the only change you make is to the attendee list, Outlook gives you the option of sending an update only to the affected attendees.

➤ **To set calendar item importance**

➜ On the item-specific tab of the item window, in the **Tags** group, click the **High Importance** button or **Low Importance** button.

➜ In the **Calendar** pane, select the item. On the item-specific tool tab, in the **Tags** group, click the **High Importance** button or **Low Importance** button.

> **Tip** If you set the importance of a single occurrence of a recurring item, the High Importance and Low Importance buttons are unavailable in the Calendar pane.

➤ **To configure reminders**

➜ On the item-specific tab of the item window, in the **Options** group, in the **Reminder** list, click the amount of time prior to the item start time that you want the reminder time to appear.

➜ In the **Calendar** pane, select the item. On the item-specific tool tab, in the **Options** group, in the **Reminder** list, click the amount of time prior to the item start time that you want the reminder time to appear.

➤ **To update calendar items**

1. Double-click the item on your calendar.

2. If the item is one of a series (a recurring item), click to indicate whether you want to edit the series or only the selected instance.

3. Make the changes you want, and then save the item.

4. If the item is a meeting, send the meeting update to the attendees.

Manage meeting options

When you receive a meeting request from another Outlook user, the meeting appears on your calendar with your time scheduled as Tentative. Until you respond to the meeting request, the organizer doesn't know whether you plan to attend.

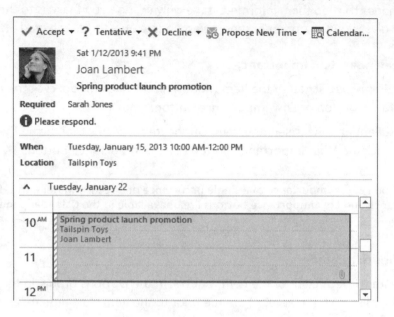

By default, meeting requests that you send include a standard set of response options. You can respond to a meeting request in one of these four ways:

- Accept the request. Outlook deletes the meeting request and adds the meeting to your calendar.

- Tentatively accept the request, which indicates that you might be able to attend the meeting but are undecided. Outlook deletes the meeting request and shows the meeting on your calendar as tentatively scheduled.

- Propose a new meeting time. Outlook sends your request to the meeting organizer for confirmation and shows the meeting with the original time on your calendar as tentatively scheduled.

- Decline the request. Outlook deletes the meeting request and removes the meeting from your calendar.

In addition to these, you have the option to reply to the meeting organizer or to all attendees, or to forward the meeting request. When you forward a meeting request for which you are not the organizer, the meeting request is sent from you "on behalf of" the meeting organizer, and responses are sent to the meeting organizer.

If you don't respond to a meeting request, the meeting remains on your calendar with your time shown as tentatively scheduled and the meeting details in gray font rather than black.

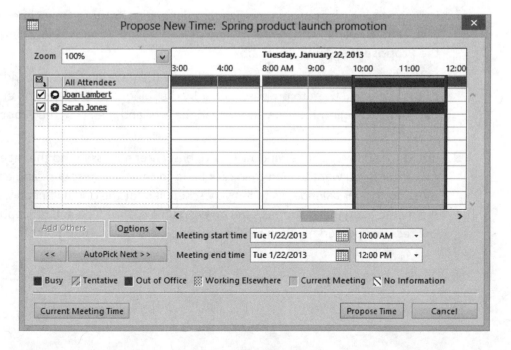

If you're unsure whether a meeting time works for you, you can click the Calendar Preview link in the meeting request to display your calendar for the time period immediately surrounding the meeting, or you can click the Calendar button at the top of the meeting request to open your default calendar for the suggested meeting day in a separate window. If the meeting time doesn't work for you, you can propose a new time.

When accepting or declining a meeting, you can choose whether to send a response to the meeting organizer. If you don't send a response, your acceptance will not be tallied, and the organizer will not know whether you are planning to attend the meeting. If you do send a response, you can add a message to the meeting organizer before sending it.

If you are the meeting organizer, you can add an attendee to a meeting at any time. If this is the only change you make to the attendee list, Outlook gives you the option of sending an update only to the new attendee.

You can take notes for any meeting in Microsoft OneNote. If you originate the notes from within the meeting request, the notes are linked to the meeting request and include all the information from the meeting request, in addition to a link back to it. If you store the notes in a shared OneNote notebook, you can make the notes available to other meeting attendees.

➤ **To respond to meeting invitations**

1. In the meeting window, in the **Reading Pane**, or on the shortcut menu that appears when you right-click the meeting request, click **Accept**, **Tentative**, or **Decline**.

2. Choose whether to send a standard response, a personalized response, or no response at all.

➤ **To propose a new time for a meeting**

1. In the meeting window or in the **Reading Pane**, click **Propose New Time**, and then click **Tentative and Propose New Time** or **Decline and Propose New Time** to open the **Propose New Time** dialog box.

2. In the **Propose New Time** dialog box, change the meeting start and end times to the times you want to propose, either by dragging the start time and end time bars or by changing the date and time in the lists, and then click the **Propose Time** button.

3. In the meeting response window that opens, enter a message to the meeting organizer if you want to, and then click **Send** to send your response and add the meeting to your calendar as tentatively scheduled for the original meeting time. If the meeting organizer approves the meeting time change, you and other attendees will receive updated meeting requests showing the new meeting time.

➤ **To forward meeting requests**

1. In the meeting window, on the **Meeting** or **Meeting Series** tab, in the **Respond** group, click the **Respond** button, and then click **Forward**.

2. Enter the recipient's email address and send the meeting request.

➤ **To add meeting participants**

1. Display the meeting window and enter new attendees by using any of the previously described methods.

2. To the left of the **To** box, click the **Send Update** button.

3. In the **Send Update to Attendees** dialog box, click **Send updates only to added or deleted attendees**, and then click **OK**.

➤ **To share meeting notes**

1. In the meeting window, on the **Meeting** or **Meeting Series** tab, in the **Meeting Notes** group, click the **Meeting Notes** button.

2. In the **Meeting Notes** window, click **Share notes with the meeting** or **Take notes on your own**.

3. In the **Choose Notes to Share with Meeting or Select Location in OneNote** dialog box, select the OneNote location in which you want to store the meeting notes, and then click **OK**.

4. Record your meeting notes in the OneNote window that opens.

➤ **To cancel meetings**

1. In the meeting window, on the **Meeting** or **Meeting Series** tab, in the **Actions** group, click the **Cancel Meeting** button.

2. In the message header, click the **Send Cancellation** button.

Practice tasks

Use the MOS Budget Meeting and MOS Status Meeting meetings that you created in section 3.2 as practice files for these tasks.

- Set a reminder for the MOS Lunch with Jane appointment to appear at 9:30 A.M.

- Reschedule the MOS Budget Meeting to the week after next, indicate that the meeting is high priority, and then send the updated meeting request.

- Ask a colleague to send you a meeting request for a meeting with the subject *MOS Project Meeting*. When the meeting request arrives, tentatively accept the meeting and propose that the meeting be held at the same time on the following day.

- From the meeting window, create a shared notes page for the MOS Project Meeting in OneNote.

- Cancel the MOS Status Meeting and MOS Budget Meeting meetings and send cancellation notices to the attendees.

3.4 Create and manage notes, tasks, and journals

Create tasks

If you use your Outlook task list to its fullest potential, you'll frequently add tasks to it. You can create tasks in several ways:

- In the Tasks module, add a task to the task list.
- In other modules, add a task to the Tasks peek.
- Create a new task in the task window.
- Base a task on an existing Outlook item (such as a message).

Just as you can create recurring appointments, events, and meetings, you can create recurring tasks. You can set the task to occur every day, week, month, or year; or you can specify that a new task should be generated a certain amount of time after the last task is complete.

Regardless of how or where you create a task, all tasks are available in the Tasks module and in the Tasks peek. Only individual tasks are available in the Tasks List.

You might frequently need to take action based on information you receive in Outlook—for example, information in a message or in a meeting request. You might want to add information from another Outlook item to your task list, to ensure that you complete any necessary follow-up work. Depending on the method you use, you can either create a new task from an existing item or simply transfer the existing item to your task list by flagging it.

> **Tip** When viewing your calendar in Day, Work Week, or Week view, each item on your Outlook task list appears in the Tasks section below its due date. You can schedule specific time to complete a task by dragging it from the Tasks area to your calendar.

➤ **To create a task in the Tasks module**

→ On the **Home** tab, in the **New** group, click the **New Task** button. Enter the task details in the task window that opens, and then save and close the task.

→ When displaying the **To-Do List** view of the Tasks module, enter the task description in the **Type a new task** box, and then press **Enter** to create a task with the default settings.

→ When displaying the **Tasks List** view of the Tasks module, enter the task description in the **Click here to add a new Task** box, press **Tab** to move to subsequent fields, fill in other information, and then press **Enter**.

➤ **To create a task in any module**

→ On the **Home** tab, in the **New** group, in the **New Items** list, click **Task**.

→ Press **Ctrl+K**.

→ In the **Tasks** peek, enter the task description in the **Type a new task** box.

➤ **To create a task from an email message, contact record, or note**

→ Drag the message, contact record, or note to the **Tasks** button on the **Navigation Bar**. Close and save the task window that contains the information from the original item.

➤ **To transfer an email message to your task list without creating an individual task**

→ In the **Mail** pane, click the flag icon to the right of a message.

This method, referred to as *flagging a message for follow-up*, adds the message to your task lists with the default due date specified in the Quick Click settings, and adds an information bar to the message. However, it does not create a separate task item, so to retain the task, you must retain the message—you can move the message between mail folders, but deleting the message deletes the task as well.

→ In the **Mail** pane, right-click the flag icon to the right of a message, and then specify a due date: **Today**, **Tomorrow**, **This Week**, **Next Week**, **No Date**, or **Custom** (which allows you to set specific start and end dates).

→ Drag the message to the **Tasks** peek and drop it under the heading for the due date you want to assign it to. (If the desired due date doesn't already have a heading in the **Tasks** peek, you need to drop the message under another heading and then assign the due date you want.)

This method also adds the message to your task list but doesn't create a separate task item.

Manage tasks

To help you organize your tasks, you can assign them to color categories in the same way that you do any other Outlook item.

When you create a task item, the only information you must include is the subject. As with many other types of Outlook items, you can set several options for tasks to make it easier to organize and identify tasks.

- **Start date and due date** You can display tasks on either the start date or the due date in the various Outlook task lists. The color of the task flag indicates the due date.

- **Status** You can track the status of a task to remind yourself of your progress. Specific status options include Not Started, In Progress, Completed, Waiting On Someone Else, or Deferred. You also have the option of indicating what percentage of the task is complete. Setting the percentage complete to 25%, 50%, or 75% sets the task status to In Progress. Setting it to 100% sets the task status to Complete.

- **Priority** Unless you indicate otherwise, a task is created with a Normal priority level. You can set the priority to add a visual indicator of a task's importance. The Low Importance setting displays a blue downward-pointing arrow, and the High Importance setting displays a red exclamation point. You can sort and filter tasks based on their priority.

- **Recurrence** You can set a task to recur on a regular basis; for example, you might create a Payroll task that recurs every month. Only the current instance of a recurring task appears in your task list. When you mark the current task as complete, Outlook creates the next instance of the task.

- **Category** Tasks use the same category list as other Outlook items. You can assign a task to a category to associate it with related items such as messages and appointments.

- **Reminder** You can set a reminder for a task in the same way you do for an appointment. The reminder appears until you dismiss it or mark the task as complete.

- **Privacy** Marking a task as private ensures that other Outlook users to whom you delegate account access can't see the task details.

None of the options are required, but they can be helpful when sorting, filtering, and prioritizing your tasks.

To track tasks to completion, you can update the Status and % Complete settings in the task window.

> **Tip** You can attach files to tasks, and you can include text, tables, charts, illustrations, hyperlinks, and other content in the task window content pane.

You can remove a task from your active task list by marking it as complete, or by deleting it. You can remove a flagged item from the active task list by removing the follow-up flag.

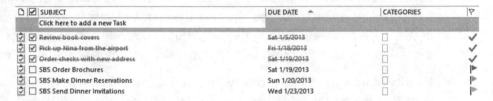

After you mark an instance of a recurring task as complete, Outlook generates a new instance of the task at whatever interval you specified when creating the task.

Removing the flag from a flagged item such as a message or contact record retains the item in its original location but removes it from your task list entirely.

➤ **To create a recurring task**

1. On the **Task** tab of the task window, in the **Recurrence** group, click the **Recurrence** button.

2. In the **Task Recurrence** dialog box, select the **Recurrence pattern** and **Range of recurrence** options you want, and then click **OK**.

➤ **To assign a task to a category**

→ In your **To-Do List** or **Tasks** peek, right-click the category icon to the right of the task subject in the task list, click **Categorize**, and then click the category you want.

→ Click the task in your **Tasks List** to select it. On the **Home** tab, in the **Tags** group, click the **Categorize** button, and then click the category you want.

→ On the **Task** tab of the task window, in the **Tags** group, click the **Categorize** button, and then click the category you want.

➤ **To assign a due date to a task**

→ In your **To-Do List** or **Tasks** peek, right-click the flag icon, and then click the due date you want.

➤ **To mark a task as private**

→ On the **Task** tab of the task window, in the **Tags** group, click the **Private** button.

➤ **To mark a task as complete**

→ In the task window, set **% Complete** to **100%**.

→ On the **Task** tab of the task window, in the **Manage Task** group, click the **Mark Complete** button.

➤ **To delete a task**

→ In your **To-Do List** or **Tasks** peek, right-click the task subject, and then click **Delete**.

→ On the **Task** tab of the task window, in the **Actions** group, click the **Delete** button.

→ In the Tasks module, in the **To-Do List** or **Tasks List**, click the flagged item to select it. Then on the **Home** tab, in the **Delete** group, click the **Delete** button.

➤ **To remove a follow-up flag**

→ Display the Tasks module, click the flagged item to select it, and then click the **Remove from List** button in the **Manage Tasks** group on the **Home** tab.

→ Click the flagged item in the **Tasks** peek, and then click the **Remove from List** button in the **Manage Tasks** group on the **Task List** tool tab.

→ Right-click the flagged item, click **Follow-up**, and then click **Clear Flag**.

Create and manage notes

In the Notes module, you can create and store text notes about any subject. If your organization uses Exchange Server, the notes are available to you whenever you connect to your account through Outlook, through your Internet browser, or from a mobile device.

> **Tip** Outlook Notes support plain text, formatted text, and hyperlinks. You can't format text within a note but you can paste formatted text from a document, message, or other source into a note and retain its formatting.

Some functionality of the Notes feature in Outlook 2013 has been modified from that of previous versions, as follows:

- The Notes folder is still available in the Folder List, and the Notes module is available from the Navigation Bar.

- Notes options are not available in the Outlook Options dialog box. You can create new notes, but only with the default color and font settings. (The note color does change to reflect any color categories that you assign to it.)

- Linking from a note to a contact record is no longer possible; however, you can attach a note to a contact record from within the contact record.

You can view the content of the Notes module in three standard views:

- **Icon view** This view depicts each note as a colored square with a turned up corner, reminiscent of a pad of sticky notes.

  In Icon view, you can display large icons organized in rows and columns, or small icons organized either in rows or in columns.

- **Notes List view** This list view displays a small icon, the note subject, and up to three lines of note content.

- **Last 7 Days view** This view is identical to Notes List view but displays only notes that have been modified within the last seven days.

In either list view, you can choose from two standard arrangements: Categories and Created Date. As with other list views, you can sort notes by a specific field by clicking the column header for that field, and you can add or remove fields from the list view.

> **Tip** The first line of text in the note is shown as its subject.

You can organize notes by assigning them to color categories. In Icon view, uncategorized notes are depicted in the default color set in the Outlook Options window; categorized notes are depicted in the most recently assigned category color. You can also attach notes to other Outlook items, such as contact records.

➤ **To create notes**

→ In the Notes module, on the **Home** tab, in the **New** group, click the **New Note** button or press **Ctrl+N.**

→ In any module, press **Ctrl+Shift+N.**

> **Tip** In Outlook 2013, Notes are not included on the New Items menu of other modules.

➤ **To assign one or more notes to a color category**

1. In the **Notes** pane, select the note or notes you want to assign to the same category.

2. On the **Home** tab, in the **Tags** group, click the **Categorize** button and then, in the list, click the category you want to assign.

➤ **To attach a note to a contact record**

1. Open the contact record window.

2. On the **Insert** tab, in the **Include** group, click **Outlook Item.**

3. In the **Insert Item** dialog box, in **the Look in** list, click the **Notes** folder, and then, in the **Items** list, click the note you want to attach.

4. In the **Insert as** area, do one of the following:

   ○ To insert the note content in the **Notes** pane of the contact record, click **Text only.**

   ○ To attach the note in the **Notes** pane of the contact record, click **Attachment.**

   ○ To create a link to the note in the **Notes** pane of the contact record, click **Shortcut.**

5. In the **Insert Item** dialog box, click **OK.**

Create journal entries

The Outlook Journal feature provides an interface through which you can track, on a timeline, interactions with a specific contact.

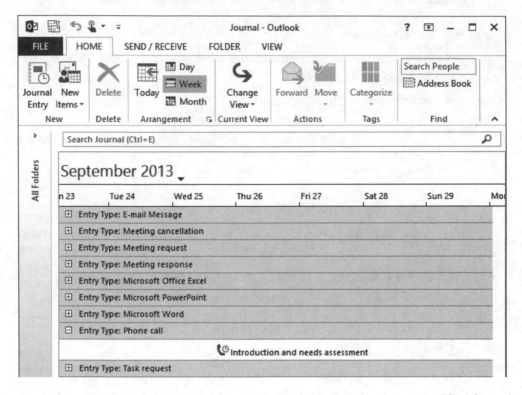

Some functionality of the Journal feature in Outlook 2013 has been modified from that of previous versions, as follows:

- The Journal folder is still available in the Folder List, but is not available from the Navigation Bar.

- Journal options are not available in the Outlook Options dialog box.

- The automatic journaling functionality has been disabled. You can still create journal entries manually.

To display the Journal module

→ On the **Navigation Bar**, click **Folders**. Then in the **Folder List**, click **Journal**.

→ Press **Ctrl+8**.

To create a journal entry

1. In the Journal module, on the **Home** tab, in the **New** group, click the **Journal Entry** button or press **Ctrl+N**.

2. On the **Journal Entry** tab, in the **Timer** group, click the **Start Timer** button if you intend to time the interaction.

3. Enter a description in the **Subject** box, and then, in the **Entry type** list, select a transaction type.

4. Enter any additional notes.

5. When you complete the journal entry, stop the timer if it was running. Then in the **Actions** group, click the **Save & Close** button.

Practice tasks

There are no practice files for these tasks.

- From the To-Do Bar, create a task with the subject *MOS Dinner Reservations*, flag it for completion this week, and assign it to the Management category (or another category you choose).

- Open a new task window, and create a task with the subject *MOS Send Dinner Invitations*. Set a due date of next Tuesday with a reminder at 5:00 P.M., and then set the status to Waiting On Someone Else.

- Open the MOS Dinner Reservations task, mark it as private and high priority, and then set it to 25 percent complete.

- Create a new task with the subject *MOS Status Report* that must be carried out on the first Monday of every month for six months.

- In the Notes module, create a note that contains your full name.

- Modify the note content so that only your first name appears as the note subject, and your last name is in the note body.

- If you haven't already done so, create a color category named *MOS*. Assign the note to the MOS color category.

- If you haven't already done so, create a contact record for yourself. Attach the note to your contact record.

Objective review

Before finishing this chapter, ensure that you have mastered the following skills:

3.1 Create and manage calendars

3.2 Create appointments, meetings, and events

3.3 Organize and manage appointments, meetings, and events

3.4 Create and manage notes, tasks, and journals

4 Manage contacts and groups

The skills tested in this section of the Microsoft Office Specialist exam for Microsoft Outlook 2013 relate to the storage and management of information about people. Specifically, the following objectives are associated with this set of skills:

4.1 Create and manage contacts

4.2 Create and manage groups

Having immediate access to current, accurate contact information for the people you need to interact with—by email, phone, mail, or otherwise—is important for timely and effective communication.

You can easily build and maintain a detailed contact list, or address book, in the Outlook People module. Within each address book, you can create contact records for individuals or companies that store various types of information about people with whom you correspond, such as business associates, customers, suppliers, family members, and friends. From your address book, you can look up information, create email messages, and schedule meetings. You can share stored contact information with other people.

To simplify communication with multiple contacts. Contact groups can consist of existing and new contacts, and can also store notes about the group.

This chapter guides you in studying ways of storing contact information for people and for groups of people you want to communicate with by email or other electronic means.

> **Practice File** To complete the practice tasks in this chapter, you need the practice file contained in the MOSOutlook2013\Objective4 practice file folder. For more information, see "Download the practice files" in this book's Introduction.

4.1 Create and manage contacts

Create and modify contact records

You save contact information for people and companies by creating a contact record in an address book.

A contact record has multiple pages. Most of the information is stored on the General page. You change pages by clicking the buttons in the Show group on the Contact tab.

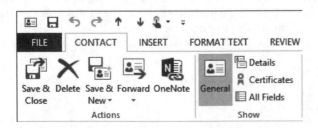

> **Strategy** When the contact record window is less than 940 pixels wide, the Show group is compacted into a button. Be sure you investigate the commands in each group.

On the General page of a contact record, you can store the following types of contact information:

- Name, company name, and job title
- Business, home, and alternate addresses
- Business, home, mobile, pager, and other phone numbers
- Business, home, and alternate fax numbers
- Webpage address (URL), instant messaging (IM) address, and up to three email addresses

> **Tip** If you need to store more than three email addresses for a contact, you can do so by creating a custom contact record form.

- Photo, company logo, or other identifying image
- General notes, which can include text and illustrations such as photos, clip art images, SmartArt diagrams, charts, and shapes

On the Details page of a contact record, you can store personal and organization-specific details, such as the following:

- Professional information, including department, office location, profession, manager's name, and assistant's name
- Personal information, including nickname, spouse or partner's name, birthday, anniversary, and the title (such as Miss, Mrs., or Ms.) and suffix (such as Jr. or Sr.) for use in correspondence

You typically create a contact record by displaying the address book to which you want to add the contact record in the People module and then clicking the New Contact button in the New group on the Home tab. In the contact record window that opens, you insert the information you want to save. After you save the contact record, it appears in the contact list.

You can create a contact record that contains only one piece of information (for example, a person's name or a company name), or as much information as you want to include. You can quickly create contact records for several people who work for the same company by cloning the company information from an existing record to a new one. And, of course, you can add to or change the information stored in a contact record at any time.

The order in which Outlook displays contact records in the contact list is controlled by the File As setting. By default, Outlook files contacts by last name (Last, First order). If you prefer, you can change the order for new contacts to any of the following:

- First Last
- Company
- Last, First (Company)
- Company (Last, First)

> **See Also** In addition to creating individual contact records, you can create groups of contacts so that you can manage messaging to multiple people through one email address. For information, see section 4.2, "Create and manage groups."

Within each contact record window, information appears not only in the fields of the contact record but also in the form of a graphic that resembles a business card. When you enter a person's contact information in a contact record, basic information appears in the business card shown in the upper-right corner of the contact window. This data includes the person's name, company, and job title; work, mobile, and home phone numbers; and email, postal, webpage, and instant messaging addresses. (Only the first 10 lines of information fit on the card.) If an image is associated with the person through Microsoft Exchange Server, SharePoint, or a social network to which you've connected Outlook, the contact record includes the image. An image from a social network is identified by a small icon in the lower-right corner of the image. You can change the types of information that appear, rearrange the information fields, format the text and background, and add, change, or remove images, such as a logo or photograph.

Creating a business card for yourself provides you with an attractive way of presenting your contact information to people you correspond with in email. You can attach your business card to an outgoing email message or include it as part (or all) of your email signature. The recipient of your business card can easily create a contact record for you by saving the business card to his or her Outlook address book.

> **See Also** For information about email signatures, see section 1.2, "Automate Outlook."

➤ **To create a new contact record**

  1. Open a new contact record window by doing any of the following:

  ○ In the People module, on the **Home** tab, in the **New** group, click the **New Contact** button.

  ○ In any module, on the **Home** tab, in the **New** group, click the **New Items** button, and then click **Contact**.

  ○ In any module, press **Ctrl+Shift+C**.

  2. Enter at least one piece of identifying information for the contact.

  3. On the **Contact** tab, in the **Actions** group, click the **Save & Close** button.

➤ **To create a contact record based on an existing contact record**

  → Open the contact record window. On the **Home** tab, in the **Actions** group, click the **Save & New** arrow, and then click **Contact from the Same Company**.

> **Troubleshooting** Double-clicking a contact in People view displays the contact information in a People card rather than in a contact record window. You cannot create a duplicate contact record from a People card. Double-clicking a contact in any view other than People view displays the contact information in a contact record window.

➤ **To create a contact record for a message sender or recipient**

  → In the **Reading Pane** or in the message reading window, right-click the message sender or recipient in the message header, and then click **Add to Outlook Contacts**.

➤ **To edit a contact record**

  → To edit a contact record from the People module, do either of the following:

  ○ In **People** view, in the **Reading Pane**, click the **Edit** link.

  ○ In any view of the People module, double-click the contact.

  → To edit a contact record from the Mail module, in the **Reading Pane**, right-click the message sender or recipient in the message header, and then click **Edit Contact**.

  → To edit a contact record from a message reading window, right-click the message sender or recipient in the message header, and then click **Edit Contact**.

➤ **To add an image to a contact record**

1. In the contact record window, on the **Contact** tab, in the **Options** group, click **Picture**, and then click **Add Picture**.

2. In the **Add Contact Picture** window, browse to and select the picture you want to attach to the contact record, and then click **Open**.

➤ **To change a contact record image**

1. In the contact record window, on the **Contact** tab, in the **Options** group, click **Picture**, and then click **Change Picture**.

2. In the **Change Contact Picture** window, browse to and select the picture you want to attach to the contact record, and then click **Open**.

➤ **To remove a contact record image**

➜ In the contact record window, on the **Contact** tab, in the **Options** group, click **Picture**, and then click **Remove Picture**.

➤ **To assign a contact record to a category**

➜ Select the contact record. On the **Home** tab, in the **Tags** group, click **Categorize**, and then click the category you want to assign.

➤ **To set the filing order for all contact records**

➜ On the **People** page of the **Outlook Options** dialog box, click the **Default "File As" Order** arrow and then, in the list, click the order you want.

➤ **To set the filing order for an individual contact record**

➜ Open the contact record. In the **File As** list, click **First Last**; **Company**; **Last, First (Company)**; or **Company (Last, First)**.

➤ **To delete a contact record**

➜ In the address book, select the contact record, and then do any of the following:

  ○ Press the **Delete** key.

  ○ On the **Home** tab, in the **Delete** group, click the **Delete** button.

  ○ Press **Ctrl+D**.

Store contact records

Contact records are stored in address books. When you configure Outlook to connect to an email account, you automatically have a default address book, which Outlook displays when you click the People button on the Navigation Bar. The default address book content is stored in a folder named *Contacts*. If you connect to an Exchange Server account, the default address book is part of that account, and the information you store in the address book is available on all computers and devices from which you connect to your account.

You display and work with address books in the People module. The content pane of the People module displays the contact records saved in the currently selected address book. The default view of contact records in Outlook 2013 is a new format named People cards, but you can choose from several standard views, including business cards, text-only cards, and various lists.

People cards display selected contact information compiled from the contact records you store in Outlook and any social networks you connect to.

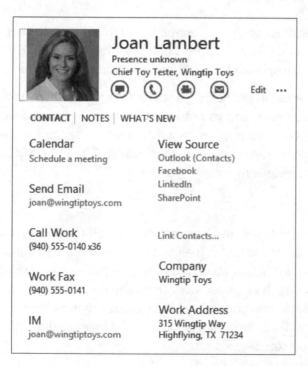

Contacts address books

Outlook creates a Contacts address book for each account and social network you connect to. These address books are available from the My Contacts list in the Folder Pane of the People module.

The Contacts address book of your default email account is your main address book, and it is the address book that appears by default in the People module. The Contacts address book is empty until you add contact records to it.

Custom address books

You can create additional address books; for example, you might want to keep contact information for family and friends in an address book separate from client contact information, or you might maintain an address book for clients that meet specific criteria.

When you display the Folder List in the Folder Pane, your custom address books appear along with other folders you create, and you can organize them in the same manner—for example, at the same level as your Inbox, as a subfolder of the Contacts address book, or inside a project folder. All address books are available from the My Contacts list in the Folder Pane of the People module.

Global Address Lists

If you have an Exchange account, you also have access to an official address book called the Global Address List (or *GAL*). The GAL is maintained by your organization's Exchange administrator and includes information about individuals within your organization, distribution lists, and resources (such as conference rooms and media equipment) that you can reserve when you schedule meetings. It can also include organizational information (each person's manager and direct subordinates) and group membership information (the distribution lists each person belongs to).

The GAL doesn't appear in the My Contacts list shown in the Folder Pane of the People module. Outlook users can view the GAL but not change its contents. Only an Exchange administrator can modify the GAL.

➤ **To create a custom address book**

1. Display the **Folder** tab of any module.

2. In the **New** group, click the **New Folder** button (or press **Ctrl+Shift+E**).

3. In the **Create New Folder** dialog box, do the following, and then click **OK**:

   a. In the **Name** box, enter a descriptive name for the address book.

   b. In the **Folder contains** list, click **Contact Items**.

   c. In the **Select where to place the folder** box, click your primary address book, if you want to store all address books in one directory structure, or any other location in which you want to store the new address book.

➤ **To add a social network address book to your My Contacts list**

1. Below the **My Contacts** list, click the **Connect to a social network** link.

2. In the **Microsoft Office** dialog box, click the social network you want to connect to.

3. In the **Settings** dialog box, do the following, and then click **OK**:

   a. Enter your user name and password for the social network.

   b. Click the **Options** button if that section is not already expanded.

   c. In the **Options** area of the dialog box, specify whether to download contacts from the social network, access social network updates, or display photos and information from your contacts' social network accounts in Outlook.

➤ **To display an address book in the People module**

→ In the **My Contacts** list, click the address book you want to display.

➤ **To display the GAL**

→ In the People module, on the **Home** tab, in the **Find** group, click the **Address Book** button.

→ In a message composition window, on the **Message** tab, in the **Names** group, click the **Address Book** button.

Share contact records and address books

You can send individual contact records to other people in an Outlook-specific format or as a vCard file (a virtual business card). You can send a contact group only in the Outlook-specific format, so the recipient must be another Outlook user.

If you want share to the contents of a custom address book with other people, you can do so by sending a sharing invitation. If the other people are within your Exchange organization, you have the option of allowing the other users to update the contact records in the address book.

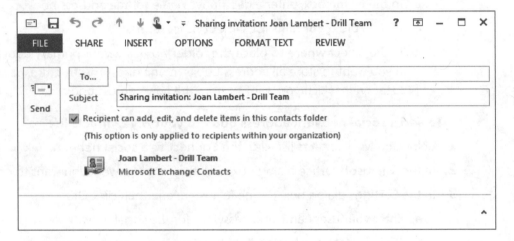

Another way to share contact information is by importing contact records from external files or locations, and exporting contact records to send to other people.

You can import data into Outlook from data files created in Outlook (.pst files) or from plain-text files that contain field values separated by commas (.csv files). Similarly, you can export contact records from Outlook in those same formats so that other people can import them into Outlook or another program.

Your organization's Microsoft SharePoint site might include contact information for employees, project team members, or other groups of people. You can import the information stored in a SharePoint contact list into Outlook as an Outlook contact folder. When you do so, Outlook creates an address book, named for the SharePoint site and contact list, that contains contact records created from the information stored in the SharePoint contact list. The new address book is available in the People module. Changes that you make to the contact records in the Outlook address book are automatically synchronized with the SharePoint contact list, and vice versa.

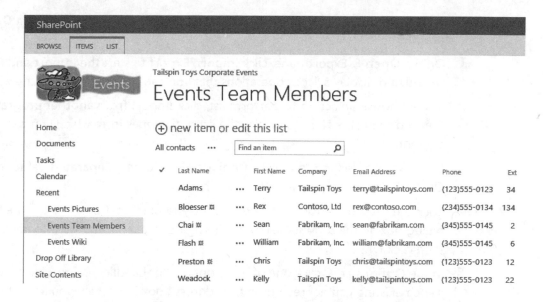

> ## To send a contact record or contact group record by email

➜ Right-click the contact or contact group, click **Forward Contact**, and then click **As a Business Card** or **As an Outlook Contact**.

> ## To share an address book

1. In the **My Contacts** list, right-click the address book, click **Share**, and then click **Share Contacts**.

   Or

   Display the address book. On the **Folder** tab, in the **Share** group, click the **Share Contacts** button.

2. In the **Sharing Invitation** message window that opens, do the following, and then click **Send**:

   a. In the **To** box, enter the email addresses of the people with whom you want to share the address book.

   b. If you want to allow other people to modify the address book content, select the **Recipient can add, edit, and delete items in this contacts folder** check box.

➤ **To import contact records from a comma-separated values file or an Outlook data file**

1. On the **Open & Export** page, click **Import/Export** to start the **Import and Export** wizard and display a list of operations that you can perform by using the wizard.

2. In the **Choose an action to perform** list, click **Import from another program or file**, and then click **Next** to display the list of file types from which you can import content.

3. In the **Select file type to import from** list, click **Comma Separated Values** or **Outlook Data File (.pst)**, and then click **Next**.

4. Click the **Browse** button to the right of the **File to import** box to open the **Browse** dialog box. In the **Browse** dialog box, navigate to the file you want to import, and then click **OK**.

5. In the **Options** area, click one of these options for handling contact records that match existing contact records in the address book into which you import them:

   ○ **Replace duplicates with items imported**

   ○ **Allow duplicates to be created**

   ○ **Do not import duplicate items**

6. Click **Next** to display a list of the folders in your Outlook installation.

7. In the **Select destination folder** list, click the address book into which you want to import the contact records, and then click **Next**.

8. If the fields defined in the file you're importing might not use the same field names as an Outlook contact record, click the **Map Custom Fields** button. Then in the **Map Custom Fields** dialog box, match named fields from the source file to Outlook field names. When you finish, click **OK**.

9. On the last page of the **Import a File** wizard, click **Finish** to import the contact records into the selected address book.

➤ **To import contact records from a source file type other than .csv or .pst**

→ Export the contact records from the source file to a .csv file, and then import the .csv file.

➤ **To import a SharePoint contact list as an address book**

1. On your organization's SharePoint site, display the contact list you want to work with.

2. Follow the correct step based on the version of SharePoint your organization is running:

    ○ In SharePoint 2013 or SharePoint 2010: on the **List** tool tab, in the **Connect & Export** group, click the **Connect to Outlook** button.

    ○ In SharePoint 2007 or SharePoint 2003: on the **Actions** menu at the top of the content pane, click **Connect to Outlook**.

3. In the **Internet Explorer** dialog box and/or **Internet Explorer Security** dialog box that opens, click **Allow** to give explicit permission for SharePoint to access Outlook.

4. In the **Microsoft Outlook** dialog box asking you to confirm that you want to connect the SharePoint document library to Outlook, click **Advanced** to open the **SharePoint List Options** dialog box.

5. Select or clear the **Display this list on other computers with the account** check box, as follows:

    ○ To download a local copy of the document library to every computer on which Outlook is configured to connect to the specified account, select the check box.

    ○ To download the document library only to the computer you're currently using, clear the check box.

6. Select or clear the **Update this subscription with the publisher's recommendation** check box, as follows:

    ○ To have the site publisher control updates, select the check box.

    ○ To manually control updates, clear the check box.

7. In the **SharePoint List Options** dialog box, click **OK**. Then in the **Microsoft Outlook** dialog box, click **Yes**. If a **Windows Security** or **Connect** dialog box appears, prompting you for your SharePoint site credentials, enter your SharePoint site user name and password, and then click **OK**.

➤ **To import contact records into a separate address book**

→ First create the address book. Then import the contact records and specify the address book as the import location.

➤ **To export contact records to a comma-separated values file**

1. On the **Open & Export** page of the **Backstage** view, click **Import/Export** to start the **Import and Export** wizard.

2. In the **Choose an action to perform** list, click **Export to a file**, and then click **Next**.

3. In the **Create a file of type** list, click **Comma Separated Values**, and then click **Next**.

4. In the **Select the folder to export from** list, click the address book from which you want to export records, and then click **Next**.

5. To the right of the **Save exported file as** box, click the **Browse** button. In the **Browse** dialog box, open the folder in which you want to save the .csv file. Enter a name for the exported file in the **File name** box, click **OK**, and then click **Next**.

6. On the last page of the wizard, click **Finish** to create the file.

➤ **To export contact records to an Outlook data file**

1. On the **Open & Export** page of the **Backstage** view, click **Import/Export** to start the **Import and Export** wizard.

2. In the **Choose an action to perform** list, click **Export to a file**, and then click **Next**.

3. In the **Create a file of type** list, click **Outlook Data File (.pst)**, and then click **Next**.

4. In the **Select the folder to export from** list, click the address book from which you want to export records.

5. If you want to export only some of the contact records from the address book, click **Filter** to open the **Filter** dialog box, filter the address book to display only the records you want to export, and then click **OK**.

6. In the **Export Outlook Data File** wizard, click **Next**.

7. To the right of the **Save exported file as** box, click the **Browse** button. In the **Open Outlook Data Files** dialog box, open the folder in which you want to save the .pst file. Enter a name for the exported file in the **File name** box, click **OK**, and then click **Next**.

> **Tip** If other data files exist in the Open Outlook Data Files dialog box, the File Name box will automatically display the name of an existing file. You must replace that file name or the previous file will be overwritten.

8. On the last page of the wizard, click **Finish**.

9. In the **Create Outlook Data File** dialog box, if you want to password-protect the file, enter a password in the **Password** and **Verify Password** boxes. Then click **OK** to create the file.

Practice tasks

The practice file for these tasks is located in the MOSOutlook2013\Objective4 practice file folder. Save the results of the tasks in the same folder.

- Create a contact record for John Evans, the Assembly Plant Manager of Wingtip Toys, which is located at 315 Wingtip Way, Highflying, TX 71234. John's email address is *john@wingtiptoys.com*, and the company website's URL is *www.wingtiptoys.com*.

- Add the *Outlook_4-1* image to the John Evans contact record.

- Create a contact record, based on the John Evans contact record, for Heidi Steen, a Sales Associate for Wingtip Toys, whose email address is *heidi@wingtiptoys.com*.

- Edit the John Evans contact record so that it is filed as *John Evans* instead of *Evans, John*. Then note that John's nickname is *Jack*, his spouse's name is *Jill*, and his birthday is *July 31*.

- If you haven't already done so, create a contact record for yourself. Include your name, company, job title, business and mobile phone numbers, fax number, one or more email addresses, and one or more postal addresses.

- Forward your contact record to a friend as a vCard. Enter *MOS Contact Information* as the message subject, and embed your business card as a signature.

- Create an address book named *MOS Contacts* that is stored within your default Contacts folder. Move the John Evans and Heidi Steen contact records to the new address book.

- Share the MOS Contacts address book with a friend. Ensure that the friend can display, but not change, the contact records in the shared address book.

- Export the MOS Contacts address book as a comma-separated values file named *MOSContacts.csv*.

4.2 Create and manage groups

If you frequently send messages to specific groups of people, such as members of a project team, club, or family, you can create a contact group that contains all the email addresses. Then you can send a message to all the group members by addressing it to the contact group.

Contact groups are like personal versions of distribution lists. A distribution list is available to everyone on your Exchange Server network; a contact group is available only from the local address book you store it in. You can, however, distribute a contact group to other people for their own use.

The ribbon provides a separate tab of commands for managing contact groups.

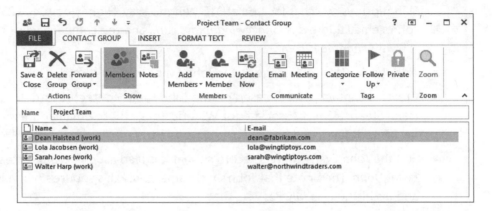

You add a member to a contact group either by selecting an existing contact record from an address book or by entering contact information in the Add New Member dialog box. When you add a member by using the latter method, you have the option to simultaneously create a contact record for him or her.

When you send a message to a contact group, each member of the contact group receives a copy of the message. If you want to send a message to most, but not all, members of a contact group, you can expand the contact group in the address field to a full list of its members, and remove individual people for the specific message at the time you send it.

➤ **To create a contact group**

1. Open a new contact group record window by doing any of the following:

   ○ In the People module, on the **Home** tab, in the **New** group, click the **New Contact Group** button.

   ○ In any module, on the **Home** tab, in the **New** group, click the **New Items** button, and then click **Contact Group**.

   ○ In any module, press **Ctrl+Shift+L**.

2. In the **Name** box, enter a name for the contact group.

3. On the **Contact Group** tab, in the **Actions** group, click the **Save & Close** button.

➤ **To open a contact group for editing**

→ In the **People Pane**, double-click the contact group to open it in a contact group window.

➤ **To add members to an open contact group**

1. On the **Contact Group** tab, in the **Members** group, click the **Add Members** button, and then click **From Address Book**.

2. In the **Select Members** dialog box, in the **Address Book** list, click the address book from which you want to add one or more contacts.

3. In the **Name** list, double-click the name of each contact you want to add.

4. In the **Select Members** dialog box, click **OK**.

   Or

1. On the **Contact Group** tab, in the **Members** group, click the **Add Members** button, and then click **New E-mail Contact**.

2. In the **Add New Member** dialog box, enter information in the **Display name** and **E-mail address** fields.

3. If you want Outlook to also create a contact record for this person, select the **Add to Contacts** check box.

4. In the **Add New Member** dialog box, click **OK**.

➤ **To remove members from a contact group**

1. Open the contact group window.

2. In the contact group member list, click the contact you want to remove.

> **Tip** You can select multiple contacts for simultaneous removal by holding down the Ctrl key and clicking each contact.

3. On the **Contact Group** tab, in the **Members** group, click the **Remove Member** button.

4. Save and close the contact group.

➤ **To update a member's information within a contact group**

1. Open the contact group window.

2. On the **Contact Group** tab, in the **Members** group, click the **Update Now** button.

3. Save and close the contact group.

➤ **To add notes to a contact group**

1. In the contact group window, in the **Show** group, click the **Notes** button.

2. On the **Notes** page, enter notes in the form of text, images, and other content.

➤ **To delete a contact group**

→ In the address book, select the contact group, and then do any of the following:

    ○ Press the **Delete** key.

    ○ On the **Home** tab, in the **Delete** group, click the **Delete** button.

    ○ Press **Ctrl+D**.

Practice tasks

Use the MOS Contacts address book you created in section 4.1 to complete these tasks.

- In the MOS Contacts address book, create a new contact group named *MOS Clients*, and select the John Evans contact record you created earlier in this chapter as a member. Add Heidi Steen to the contact group, and then save and close the contact group.

- Add the following people to the MOS Clients contact group and to your contact list:

  Holly Dickson holly@consolidatedmessenger.com

  Max Stevens max@consolidatedmessenger.com

  Linda Mitchell linda@lucernepublishing.com

  Jill Shrader jill@lucernepublishing.com

- Open the contact record for Jill Shrader, change her email address to *jill@wingtiptoys.com*, and then update the MOS Clients contact group to reflect Jill Shrader's new email address.

- Send a message with the subject *MOS Group Test* to the MOS Clients contact group. (You will receive nondeliverable message alerts in response.)

Objective review

Before finishing this chapter, ensure that you have mastered the following skills:

4.1 Create and manage contacts

4.2 Create and manage groups

Index

About the author

Joan Lambert has worked closely with Microsoft technologies since 1986, and in the training and certification industry since 1997. As President of Online Training Solutions, Inc. (OTSI), Joan is responsible for guiding the translation of technical information and requirements into useful, relevant, and measurable training and certification tools.

Joan is a Microsoft Certified Trainer, Microsoft Office Master, Microsoft Certified Technology Specialist, Microsoft Technology Associate, and the author of more than two dozen books about Windows and Office (for Windows and Mac). Joan enthusiastically shares her love of technology through her participation in the creation of books, learning materials, and certification exams.

Joan currently lives in a nearly perfect small town in Texas with her simply divine daughter, Trinity, two dogs, one cat, a multitude of fish, and the super-automatic espresso machine that runs the house.

Online Training Solutions, Inc. (OTSI)

OTSI specializes in the design, creation, and production of Microsoft Office, SharePoint, and Windows training products for information workers and home computer users. For more information about OTSI, visit *www.otsi.com*.

The team

This book would not exist without the support of these hard-working members of the OTSI publishing team:

- Denise Bankaitis
- Rob Carr
- Susie Carr
- Jeanne Craver
- Kathy Krause
- Marlene Lambert
- Barb Levy
- Jaime Odell
- Victoria Thulman
- Jean Trenary
- Krista Wall

We are especially thankful to the support staff at home who make it possible for our team members to devote their time and attention to these projects.

Rosemary Caperton and Valerie Woolley provided invaluable support on behalf of Microsoft Press.

Now that you've read the book...

Tell us what you think!

Was it useful?
Did it teach you what you wanted to learn?
Was there room for improvement?

Let us know at http://aka.ms/tellpress

Your feedback goes directly to the staff at Microsoft Press,
and we read every one of your responses. Thanks in advance!

 Microsoft